Presen

From:

_____

Date:

"Love the Lord your God with all your heart

and with all your soul and with all your

strength and with all your mind."

~Luke 10:27

Growing Faith. Living Hope.

"Don't let the hurts and complexities of life keep you down. Join Sarah Meece as she shares a daily nugget of hope and inspiration, straight from God's heart to yours. His Word, combined with Sarah's challenge, will give you strength to face each day, confident in His power to heal."

> ~Vonda Skelton, Founder and Co-Director, Christian Communicators Conference • *Seeing Through the Lies: Unmasking the Myths Women Believe*

"To know Sarah Meece is to know hope. She not only has the grit and determination to persevere through life and death experiences, but also maintains the insistence of being a herald of hope for the God who holds and heals her. In *A Dose of Hope*, you will experience the redemptive reflections of a woman whose vibrant faith in God and people is a testimony to the power and purpose of hope."

> ~ Dr. Dan Francis, Senior Pastor

"If there is anyone who has experienced as many life-altering storms as Sarah Meece and been able to emerge on the other side with stronger faith, hope, and joy...I haven't met that person yet. Sarah is the real deal and a role model for me in how to live out one's faith with joy in the midst of challenges. That's why the devotions in this book are so powerful. They are not written by someone who understands hope in theory. They are written by someone who has lived by hope in the midst of storms!"

> ~Kent Julian, Motivational Keynote Speaker, Speaker Coach, Author, & Founder of www.liveitforward.com

Sarah Meece

A Dose of Hope
Devotions for Healing the Heart

Eileen: What a joy to meet you! Thank you so much for calling me. You have such a lovely Spirit. Lets please keep in touch! Much love any many blessings!

Love,
Sarah

A Dose of Hope by Sarah Meece
Copyright © 2013 by Sarah Meece
All rights reserved.

Scripture References are from NIV Study Bible, 10th Anniversary Edition, 1995 by The Zondervan Corporation

Cover Design: Kari Underhill
Interior Design: Sarah Meece with Ellen Sallas, The Author's Mentor, www.theauthorsmentor.com

Golden Ridge Publishing
ISBN-13: 978-0615889313
ISBN-10: 061588931X
LCCN: 2013951434

PRINTED IN THE UNITED STATES OF AMERICA

Dedication

To My Husband, Curry:

You are truly my gift from God. Thank you for your
tremendous love and support. I am blessed beyond
measure to have you for my husband.
Thank you for always believing in me;
I love living life with you.
I love you.

To My Friend, Kathy Straub—
"Editor in Chief":

Your God-given gifts never cease to amaze me. I am
extremely thankful to you for sharing your knowledge,
expertise, and gracious heart
during the book-writing process.
Much love to you,
dear friend.

Contents

Introduction

My life journey has been an interesting one, to say the least. I have experienced a roller coaster of events that have taken me through what has seemed to be a real obstacle course beginning with the death of my mother at an early age, a devastating divorce, a murder attempt on my life, which resulted in living in hiding for many months, and most recently, breast cancer. I have certainly had my share of twists and turns, peaks and valleys, sunshine and storms. But what brought me to the joy that I live in today has been the grace of God. It is because of my faith in Him that I am a true survivor. I praise God for a family who taught me about the love of Jesus Christ because without Him, I know I could not have survived these devastating events in my life.

A Dose of Hope is a gentle reminder that regardless of the situation, we need to turn our hearts and minds toward God for survival. My purpose in writing this book is to help you build a deeper, more intimate relationship with God. As you read each devotion, the challenge question will offer an opportunity for journaling. By answering these questions, not only will this allow you to have some quiet time with God, but you will also have the opportunity to do some real soul searching. The journaling experience is designed to encourage self-evaluation and to help you deal with difficult situations in your own life. Regardless of how deeply rooted our relationships are with God, we can always grow, learn, and mature in our faith.

Within the pages of this book, it is my hope and prayer that you will find strength, comfort, encouragement, and a small **Dose of Hope.** God promises that *"he will never leave us or forsake us"* [Hebrews 13:5] and in each devotion, you will find the reassurance that no matter what obstacle you may be encountering in your life, God is always there for you, God loves you unconditionally, and He wants you to find true happiness and peace.

Enjoy **A Dose of Hope!**

May God Bless You,

Sarah

But as for me I will always have *hope.*
~Psalm 71:14

"He gives strength to the weary

*...and increases power of the weak.
Even youths grow tired and weary,
and young men stumble and fall;
but those who HOPE in the Lord,
will renew their strength.
They will soar on wings like eagles;
they will run and not grow weary,
they will walk and not be faint."
~Isaiah 40:29-31*

Dancing In The Rain

"Consider it pure joy, my brothers, whenever you face trials of many kinds, because you know that the testing of your faith develops perseverance."
~James 1:2-3

As crazy as it sounds, in many ways our lives are like the weather—changing at the drop of a hat and many times, difficult to predict. We often have sunny days filled with happy experiences and smooth sailing. Unfortunately, periodically we suffer storms consisting of difficulties, trials and temptations. Sometimes even a hurricane comes ashore and simply whisks us off our feet, tossing us into the depths of despair.

How are we supposed to persevere through these difficult conditions? We must hold steadfast to our faith, regardless of the anticipated forecast. When we have difficulty "holding on" and persevering in the midst of life's storms, we need to look to God's word as our anchor in turbulent weather. We could, perhaps, join a Bible study group to help us through the rough places, or possibly find a Christian friend who can mentor us and help us keep our heads above water while our storms are raging around us.

As Christians, we realize these storms are temporary because we have the assurance of eternal life. The rainbow at the end of the storm is God's promise of what is to come. What a comforting thought—spending eternity in heaven!

In James, we are told that we will be blessed when we persevere under trials [James 1:12]. Everyone experiences pain and tribulation at one time or another, but if we have faith and confidence in God, then He will bless us. Maybe we can take our "storm" and turn it into something positive by helping someone else who is experiencing a similar storm.

"Life is not waiting for the storm to pass; it is learning to dance in the rain!" **Let God be your dancing partner!**

Challenge of the Day

Can you recall a particular storm you experienced in your life? What have you learned from your storms?

Day 2

Jealousy: Confronting the Monster

"You are still worldly. For since there is jealousy and quarreling among you, are you not worldly?"
~1 Corinthians 3:3

Two brothers were raised in the same household by the same parents, yet they could not have been more different. One brother was ambitious, extremely career oriented, lived in a larger home, and drove a nicer car. The other brother certainly wasn't a bum on the street, but he just couldn't get past the fact that his brother appeared to be so much more successful. He was eaten alive with jealousy and, unfortunately, allowed it to destroy their relationship.

Jealousy is an extremely common emotion. It is something we have all experienced, and it can happen at any time, any place. Whether in school, in a group at church, in the workplace, or at the family dinner table, we have all encountered this situation to some degree. According to statistics, infants as early as five months old feel jealousy. The sad thing about that "green-eyed monster" is if we fail to recognize it and allow it to contaminate our relationships, jealousy can have a devastating effect on how we feel about others. Just like those brothers, that monster can devour a healthy relationship.

In his letter, Paul calls the Corinthians "infants in the Christian life" because they quarreled like children and allowed jealousy and arguing to affect the strength of their church. Isn't that exactly what jealousy does to us? When we spend our time and energy focusing on envy, we begin to resent those around us and lose the joy of relationships. It causes division.

We should try to be honest with ourselves. Learn to recognize jealousy and envy before they become monsters that destroy a precious relationship. We can pray about it and turn our focus to God. Rejoice in the good fortune of others rather than being resentful and envious; that's what God would want us to do!

Challenge of the Day

When was the last time you remember feeling jealous? Did you allow that jealousy to affect your relationship with someone? Or were you able to rejoice with them in their success?

Brokenhearted

"The Lord is close to the brokenhearted and saves those who are crushed in spirit." ~Psalm 34:18

For several weeks, the physicians had said Bob's prognosis was hopeful. His recovery would be gradual but the doctors thought eventually he would be alright. Linda was so relieved to hear those words of encouragement and hope, and she felt optimistic as they left the doctor's office. But unfortunately, it was only days before Bob suddenly passed away. It was such a shock, Linda felt betrayed—not only by the doctors, but also by God. Why hadn't the doctors done more to save her husband, and why had God let her down after all she and Bob had suffered together?

Linda was filled with complete despair. She was angry, grief-stricken, and experienced feelings of sadness, depression, and loneliness. No doubt, Linda was suffering terribly and felt cheated and brokenhearted by her loss.

For those of us left behind after our loved ones pass, we often have these feelings of devastation. We must remember that we are not alone. God is with us. If our loved one was a child of God, we know he/she is rejoicing with God in heaven, and that should be such a tremendous comfort. For those left behind to mourn, God knows our heart. In Psalm 34:18, we are reminded that God is close to the brokenhearted. He will come to our rescue; we need to have faith and allow Him to give us strength and comfort in our time of grief.

In the Bible, Jesus reassures us that our hurting hearts will be comforted after such a terrible loss. Didn't He teach us in one of His most memorable lessons on God's love, *"Blessed are those who mourn, for they shall be comforted"* [Matthew 5:4]? God is there to restore those who are broken and crushed in spirit. Mourning is a natural emotion we will all experience at some point in our lives, but we should never let it make us angry with God. Without mourning, there can be no true rejoicing!

Challenge of the Day

Have you had a reason to mourn recently? Have you felt angry with God because something happened to someone you love? Or did you turn to God and ask Him to help heal your broken heart?

Am I Ready For This?

"Have I not commanded you? Be strong and courageous. Do not be terrified;
do not be discouraged, for the LORD *your God*
will be with you wherever you go." ~Joshua 1:9

In the company's organizational chart, Aubrey was just one level below Vice President of Marketing. She had worked for this company for over 20 years and had made her way up the career ladder. After announcing the resignation of the VP, the CEO came to Aubrey asking if she would like to be promoted to fill the position. It was an incredible honor and a once-in-a-lifetime opportunity. Aubrey knew in her heart she could do the job, and yet she was filled with worry and self-doubt. Was she really ready for this huge move? She realized this new position would bring many new responsibilities, create new challenges, more stress and pressure. Aubrey's life would certainly change. "Am I ready for this?" she wondered.

Aubrey immediately thought of Joshua. Moses had Joshua as his "personal aide" for over 40 years. However, at Moses' death, Joshua found himself left with the incredible task of leading the Israelites, more than two million people! Can we imagine the overwhelming anxiety and self-doubt he must have felt? Can't we just hear him asking God the same question Aubrey asked, "Am I ready for this?"

Whether we are changing positions within a company or completely changing the direction of our life's paths, fear and self-doubt are common emotions. Most of us are afraid of change. Assuming a brand new direction in our lives can be challenging and sometimes downright frightening. Whenever we are faced with fretful emotions such as apprehension and anxiety, we need to follow the advice given to Joshua: *"Be strong and courageous, not terrified"*. We know God is with us *"wherever we go,"* regardless of the journey.

As God was with Joshua, He will be with us through our challenging decisions or difficult adjustments. God wants us to succeed as we climb our "career ladders" of life, but more importantly, God wants our hearts and minds to be intertwined with His. Maybe we can bring more to the executive boardroom than business acumen; maybe we can bring God! With Him as the CEO of our life's "corporation," we are definitely **ready for this!**

Challenge of the Day

Can you remember an instance when you were anxious about making a big change in some aspect of your life? How did you see God working in your decision-making or adjustment process? Was God part of your executive plan?

From The Inside Out

"She is clothed with strength and dignity...beauty is fleeting but a woman who fears the Lord is to be praised."
~Proverbs 31:25, 30

A recent survey found that women spend an average of $13,000 in their lifetimes on makeup and beauty aids. Really? On average, ladies shop for makeup about five times a year, spending around $40 each trip. When multiplied by 65 years, that brings us to a whopping **thirteen thousand dollars**! Even in a bad economy when they can't afford to splurge on new clothes, many women might purchase a new tube of lipstick or a new color of fingernail polish just to make themselves feel more beautiful. It's no wonder the beauty industry is practically recession proof!

Yes, making ourselves more attractive is important to most women. But we've probably all heard the old adage, "She's just as pretty on the inside as she is on the outside!" We might spend thousands of dollars creating an image of beauty, but without a heart for God, we have only created an illusion; it's just a façade.

In Proverbs 31, we are given a description of a woman of noble character. Notice the passage never mentions anything about smearing makeup on our faces to make us gorgeous. Another excellent expression of a woman's true beauty comes in 1 Peter 3:3-4 which says, *"Your beauty should not come from outward adornment, such as braided hair and the wearing of gold jewelry and fine clothes. Instead, it should be that of your inner self, the unfading beauty of a gentle and quiet spirit, which is of great worth in God's sight."* Isn't it much more important for us to be beautiful in God's eyes than in the eyes of other people?

There's certainly nothing wrong with trying to put forth an attractive appearance. But we need to look within and make sure that our true beauty comes from our hearts, not from a jar! Let's allow God's love to bring out our natural beauty because we know it's what's on the inside that counts! Then others will look at **us** and say, "She's just as pretty on the inside as she is on the outside!"

Challenge of the Day

Do you know someone who you feel is just as pretty on the inside as she is on the outside? If so, what do you think are the characteristics that make you see her that way? What can you do to make yourself more beautiful in the eyes of God?

"You Are Who You Run With"

"Do not be misled: 'Bad company corrupts good character.'"
~1 Corinthians 15:33

When Wade entered the classroom after summer vacation, his teacher noticed immediately that Wade's disposition, demeanor, and physical appearance had changed significantly. As the year progressed, she also noticed that Wade's grades were slipping. She had had him in class before and he had always been an A student. What happened in those twelve short weeks of summer vacation? After speaking with Wade's parents, she realized Wade had simply gotten involved in the "wrong crowd." Fortunately, this Christian teacher sat down with Wade and expressed her concern. In the course of their conversation, she shared with him an old saying, "You are who you run with." At the end of their discussion, she asked him a very important question, "Wade, is this who you really want to be?" He gave that some serious thought as she continued with the importance of not allowing peer pressure to get tangled up in his dreams and aspirations. She urged him not to let others determine his character, to make sure that his behavior was pleasing to God, not to his buddies!"

What happens to us when life hands us peer pressure? Have we ever found ourselves like Wade, wanting to fit in with "the crowd" so much that we were willing to compromise our values, morals, or principles just to be accepted?

Regardless of how strong we are, it is sometimes difficult to stay true to our Christian walk when we spend our time and resources in an ungodly fashion. Satan wins! When we let our behavior and ideas be influenced by those who are not believers, we need to step back, take a closer look, and make sure our hearts are in the right place; otherwise, we could wake up in the middle of a place where we don't belong. As we know from scripture, *"Bad company corrupts good character."*

Remember that old saying, **"You are who you run with!"** We need to ask ourselves, "Would God be pleased with the company I am keeping? Would He like my group of running mates?"

Challenge of the Day

Have you ever found yourself in a mess because you chose the wrong "running mates"? What were the consequences of that relationship? Do you use different criteria when you choose your friends now?

Guaranteed!

"Do not merely listen to the word, and so deceive yourself.
Do what it says." ~James 1:22

We have all seen those commercials that promise happiness and a perfect life if we use a certain product. These ads try to convince us that we can have more luxurious hair, better breath, fewer wrinkles, whiter clothes, lose two dress sizes, be the ideal mother, raise well-adjusted children, drive the car with the most advanced technology—all **guaranteed** or our money back! Marketers want us to believe their products are the best, most improved, most affordable and the healthiest for us. Their job is to persuade us to spend our hard-earned dollars on their product because they can **guarantee** that it's going to do everything they promise it will do! But can we really believe that promise?

As Christians, where do we turn to find "commercials" for Christ? We certainly won't find ads for Jesus on TV, but if we truly want to know what God has guaranteed His children, all we have to do is read the Bible and follow God's direction. When James wrote letters to the Jewish Christians, he made practical suggestions for everyday living, which is why the book of James is known as a "How To Book." He didn't make empty promises about making us perfect. He spoke the truth about how we should live each day using Christ as our example. And when Christ makes a **guarantee**, we can be sure that it comes from God Himself.

In addition, James encourages us not to just read about living a good life; we must take action! We should study what the Bible has to say to us, and then **live it**! We know that God truly does have the biggest, best, most perfect advice for us. And His **guarantee** doesn't need to come with a money-back promise. His **guarantee** is eternal life!

Challenge of the Day

Have you read the book of James lately? If not, take a few minutes and do it today. What guarantees do you find within its pages? With whom will you share your "commercial"?

Fortunately Or Unfortunately?

"In his heart a man plans his course, but the Lord determines his steps."
~Proverbs 16:9

A high school teacher once told her high achievers, "Organization is essential to success." She continued to share the importance of not only organizing their lives as it related to their material possessions, but more importantly, how being organized was essential as it related to their goals, dreams, and aspirations. Her students needed to understand the importance of organization in all aspects of their lives. Actually, we **all** need direction, structure, organization, and a well-thought-out plan for the future.

"Unfortunately," we all know the best laid plans can often go astray. Or should we say, "Fortunately"? When we have prepared for a task or goal ahead and our plans don't stay on course, how do we react? Do we get angry or frustrated and think, "Oh, this is really unfortunate" or do we set our minds in a more spiritual tone and think, "Well, maybe my original plan was not necessarily God's plan"? Do we wallow in self-pity because our well-designed, carefully mapped-out plan did not come to fruition? Or do we go to God in prayer, ask Him to be with us and await the arrival of **His** plan? Do we ever consider that perhaps God has a bigger and better plan for us? Maybe what we perceived as an unfortunate turn of events eventually becomes a fortuitous direction after all.

Often, our attitudes determine the direction our hearts go when we look back at the remnants of our mislaid plans. We may feel we have everything under control, that we are organized and know exactly where we're going. **Unfortunately**, we don't always have a full understanding of the purpose God has for us. But **fortunately**, the one thing we definitely know is that God is directing our steps. His direction is keeping us on the right path!

Challenge of the Day

Can you recall a time in your life when your plans didn't go as you had anticipated? However, when you looked back, did you realize God had a better plan for you? What did you learn from this experience?

We Need To Talk!

"But when you pray, go into your room, close the door,
and pray to your Father, who is unseen. Then your Father, who sees what is
done in secret, will reward you."
~Matthew 6:6

Katy and Josh were so excited! They had just completed the last of a series of prenuptial counseling sessions and the pastor had given them his blessing. Looking back over the topics they had discussed during their counseling, Katy and Josh agreed the lesson on the importance of communication was their favorite. They had learned that one of the most essential factors in a successful marriage was keeping the lines of communication open no matter what the circumstances might be.

Isn't that true of any relationship? Communication is one of the most important elements in all successful relationships whether it's with our friends, co-workers, children or parents, and most importantly, with God. We know God created us so He could have a relationship with us. He wants so much for us to talk to Him to discuss our concerns, our joys as well as our sorrows.

Many of us feel like we really don't know **how** to pray so we just avoid doing it. Sometimes we feel like all we have is our old standby checklist, and we tend to pray for the same things over and over again. Even then, we are at least expressing our thoughts to God and He listens. But then the question arises: Do we ever stop and listen to Him? Communication is a two-way street. We talk first, make our point, but then we don't just say, "OK, thanks for listening…Goodbye!" We should take the time after we pray to stay in that quiet place and listen for God to answer. It may take some practice but it can happen!

Prayer is not asking. It is a longing of the soul. It is a daily admission of one's weakness. It is better in prayer to have a heart without words, than words without a heart. –Mahatma Gandhi

Let us all be aware of the importance of talking to God. It is the key to keeping the lines of communication open with the One who really wants to hear what we have to say!

Challenge of the Day

Do you find it difficult to pray, thinking that you just don't know the right words? Do you ever take the time to listen for God's response when you talk to Him? Can you describe a time when you really felt God was responding to your prayer?

Charging Your Battery

"Jesus said to them, 'Come with me by yourselves to a quiet place and get some rest.'" ~Mark 6:31

"I just don't know how I'm going to get all of this done!" Katherine cried with frustration. She was at the end of her rope with so many responsibilities piling up on her plate. She just didn't know how she was going to deal with it all. With her additional hours at work, trying to meet her children's growing demands, keeping her home relatively clean, and managing her husband's ad campaign for his new company, Katherine was simply overwhelmed. She found herself so busy with everybody else's needs, she was forgetting her own!

It is easy for us to find ourselves in a situation similar to Katherine's. We can become bombarded with so many responsibilities in our everyday routines that we can lose track of our own need for spiritual renewal. Of course, it's difficult to stop in the middle of a busy day to take time for ourselves. But our relationship with God suffers when we don't take a few minutes each day to be with Him. It could be in the morning before we begin our daily chores or at night just before bed.

Whatever time we choose, we should realize the importance of keeping our spiritual batteries charged.

Pastor Rick Warren gives an excellent example of how our inner batteries work. His analogy illustrates that one light bulb can run for a long time on one battery. Put two lights on that same battery and the energy is depleted a bit faster. Add four or five bulbs and that battery is drained of energy in no time. Too many irons in the fire put out the fire! That's what happens to our own spiritual batteries when we try to do too many things with only one source of power. Wouldn't the power of God keep that battery working forever?

No matter how hectic our day may be, all the activities we're involved in can't be as important as communicating with our heavenly Father. Prioritize! We need to find time for Him in our busy schedules. Let Him recharge our spiritual batteries by finding a quiet place with Him for just a few minutes each day and get some spiritual renewal!!

Challenge of the Day

Do you ever find yourself so busy that you don't have time for God? Can you think of a time during your day when you could spend some quality time with your heavenly Father?

Day 11

Let's Make A Deal!

"Do not put the Lord your God to the test." ~*Luke 4:12*

O n her knees, Megan begged and pleaded, "Dear God, if you will help me get through this mess, I promise I will go to church every Sunday and I'll start serving you." Megan had not been a dedicated believer, but her circumstances had become so desperate that she was now playing **"Let's Make A Deal"** with God. It felt like it was her last resort.

We have probably found ourselves in a similar situation in which we may not have been as grounded in our faith as we should have been. Suddenly, we look up and our lives are in complete chaos. We see no other way out so we decide that just maybe, calling upon God for help might be our last chance. In our desperation, we try to bargain with God, making a deal with Him, thinking this will solve our problem, at least temporarily. Sad but true, Satan tempts us and often these temptations compromise our faith. When this happens, we find ourselves in the same situation as Megan—pleading with God and making rash promises we might not be able to keep. It's like wanting to see what's behind Door Number 2 and ending up with nothing!

Why do we think we can play games with God? Sometimes it's hard to believe that God loves us so much and that He is always there for us, not just when we're down to our last hope, but every second of every day. Even when we stray from our faith, He is always there to welcome us back with open arms. All we have to do is rely on God's word and stand firm in our commitment to Him. He will never leave us or desert us, even in the most desperate of times. We need to follow Jesus' example and remember the words from Psalm 121:7, *"The Lord will keep you from all harm—He will watch over your life."* Leave the deal making to the game shows on TV. We have a God whose best deal is His gift of eternal life!

Challenge of the Day

Have you played "Let's Make A Deal" with God lately? If so, what did you learn? What advice would you give to a friend who you saw playing games with God?

Guardrails Of Life

"Above all else, guard your heart,
for it is the wellspring of life."
~Proverbs 4:23

Not far from Andrea's house, there was a very dangerous stretch of road. The narrow highway made a sharp curve and there was a steep drop off near the right shoulder. Andrea always made a point to slow down when she came to that spot because there had been several accidents in which cars took the treacherous turn too fast and ended up in the ravine. A guardrail was needed there in the worst way.

In life, we often find ourselves taking dangerous, winding roads with treacherous curves and unexpected turns. If we aren't careful and don't follow God's road map, we can find ourselves down in that steep ravine. Guardrails are certainly one way of keeping us traveling in the right direction and protecting us when hazardous conditions occur on our life's highway. As we drive through our everyday lives, however, there are many times we veer off in the wrong direction and we need God's GPS to help us get back on the right road. Perhaps we "yield" to temptation and have to make a "U turn" when things get difficult. We might even have to "detour" around the obstacles in our path to make certain we are going the "one way" God intended for our journey. As long as we "go" in the right direction and obey the "speed limits" of God's plan, we won't ever have to "STOP" because of the dangerous "construction ahead." By studying God's word, we can make the correct turn at the "intersection between right and wrong" and know exactly what our heavenly destination is going to be!

If we have doubts about God's direction, take time to read the Ten Commandments. [Exodus 20] These "guardrails" from God remind us of the route we need to take in order to live our lives according to His will. No matter what obstacles we encounter on our highway of life, let's allow those Godly "guardrails" to keep us on the road to eternal life!

Challenge of the Day

Discuss a time when you lost your way and ran off the road God intended for you. Have you been able to get back on the right track? If so, how do you think you accomplished that "U turn"? If not, what can you do now to get yourself to your intended destination?

Second Chances

"Forgive as the Lord forgave you." ~Colossians 3:13

With tears rolling down her cheeks, Amy said to her friend, Lisa, "I know I've made such a mess of things and I've hurt you. I'm so sorry, Lisa. Can you ever forgive me?" Amy had made a serious mistake that damaged her relationship with one of her best friends. Now, as she realized the consequences, all she could do was beg Lisa for a second chance. She desperately needed her friend to forgive her. Lisa looked at her friend, gave her a hug and said, "How can I **not** forgive you? I'm just glad you're back!"

Let's try to picture ourselves in this little scenario. At one time or another, we've all probably been an Amy and made a bad decision that ended up hurting someone we loved. Were we able to admit our mistakes, go to that person and ask for their forgiveness? It's not an easy thing to do; we all hate to admit we've been wrong. Or have we ever been a Lisa and had to forgive someone who's really hurt us? Were we able to forgive, to give that person a second chance…even a third or fourth?

Jesus was asked, *"Lord how often should I forgive someone who sins against me? Seven times?"* Jesus replied, *"No, not seven times, but seventy times seven!"* [Matthew 18:21-22.] Lisa was simply following the teaching of Jesus when she chose to forgive Amy and give her a second chance. And what a blessing it is for **us** that we have a loving and forgiving God. He fills our lives with second chances. He's given us free will and sometimes we make mistakes, making a mess of things. But once we realize all we have to do is recognize our transgression, ask God for His mercy, grace, forgiveness and love, we are always given a second chance. Hopefully, we learn from our mistakes and those second chances make us stronger and more grounded in Christ. We need to thank God every day that we have been given so many chances to get it right!

Challenge of the Day

Have you ever asked God for a second chance? Have you been willing to give someone else a second chance when they have hurt you? Explain.

Ruby Red Lips

"Those who look to him are radiant; their faces are never covered with shame." ~Psalm 34:5

Maria took one last glance into the mirror as she hurriedly got ready for work. Suddenly, she realized she had forgotten to put on any lipstick. As she opened the tube of her favorite shade of red, she smiled as it brought back a pleasant memory. As a little girl, Maria had spent quite a bit of time with her Aunt Lorene, and she remembered watching her put on her beautiful ruby red lips every morning. She would then observe closely as her aunt pressed her lips together to make sure the lipstick color was even on both her upper and lower lips. As Aunt Lorene pressed her lips on a tissue, she would tell Maria, "When you get to be a big girl, you can put on your ruby red lips too." Maria waited anxiously for the day when she could have beautiful red lips just like her beloved aunt.

However, as Maria matured—both in age and as a Christian—she realized that ruby red lips weren't the only qualities that made a person beautiful. She had come to understand that, more important than lip color, were the words that came out of those expressive lips. In order for her to convey her love for God, her words had to reflect what was in her heart. They had to come from the Holy Spirit that lived within her. She knew that kind, loving words were much more significant than choosing the perfect shade of lipstick.

Do our words reveal to others what is truly in our heart? Do our lips speak lovingly, with kindness and a gentle spirit? Do our words reflect a heart for God and allow others to see God through us? Now that we are "big girls," we need to ask God to help us bring out our inner radiance so that our lips, no matter what shade of lipstick we are wearing, show the world that we have a true relationship with our heavenly Father. Let's make sure our "ruby red lips" reflect a true heart for God!

Challenge of the Day

What do the words from your "ruby red lips" reveal about you? If asked, what would your friends say about the words **they** hear from your "ruby red lips?"

Day 15

We've Already Won

"Where, O death, is your victory? Where, O death, is your sting?...Thanks be to God! He gives us the victory through our Lord Jesus Christ." ~1 Corinthians 15:55, 57

Sandy was a huge fan of college basketball and tonight's game was going to be more exciting than ever. Her alma mater was playing in the big semi-final game that night, and they had a great chance of going all the way to the national championship. Unfortunately, tonight she also had a mandatory meeting at work. Carefully, Sandy set the DVR on her TV so she could watch the entire game when she got home from the office.

When her meeting ended, Sandy rushed to her car so she could get home in a hurry. She knew she had probably missed the game but felt reassured, knowing her trusty DVR had recorded every minute of the game. As she drove home, she turned on her radio for some relaxing music to help calm her nerves. Suddenly, the DJ announced that Sandy's team had just won the game by a narrow margin and they were, indeed, headed for the final championship game. "That's great!" she thought. "Now I don't need to watch the game because I know how it turns out! I already know the final score!"

Of course, being the dedicated fan that she was, Sandy did watch the game when she got home, but this time, she had an entirely different attitude. Instead of the usual nail-biting, on the edge of her seat, stressed-out attitude, tonight she was completely calm, confident and relaxed as she enjoyed the game. She knew her team was going to win!

And isn't that how we as Christians should feel? Don't we already know the score of our life's "game"? Why should we be anxious and worried when we know that through His grace, God has already won the game for us through Christ's death? With faith in Jesus, we have His precious promise of eternal life. We can be confident and self-assured because we know the outcome of our "game." We've already won!

Challenge of the Day

Think about the promise of eternal life we have from God. How do you think that will change your attitude toward your life today? What changes will you make in your "game plan" now that you know the outcome?

Day 16

Life's Chalk Walk

"I know the plans I have for you," declares the Lord, "plans to prosper you and not to harm you, plans to give you hope and a future."
~Jeremiah 29:11

Little Mary Jane had used nearly an entire box of sidewalk chalk to draw a beautiful path along her grandmother's sidewalk. Utilizing a variety of colors, she had drawn a pathway filled with flowers, stars, animals, and rainbows. And of course, Mary Jane's grandmother thought she had created a magnificent masterpiece!

The following morning when Mary Jane went out to hop and skip along her beautiful pathway, she began to cry. A terrible storm had come in the night and all of her precious artwork had been destroyed. The rain had washed it all away and now there were only smudges of color all blended together. Sobbing, she ran to her grandmother for comfort.

Our lives are often a bit like chalk pathways. We use a variety of colors and we paint our paths with what we believe to be beautiful designs. We think we have the perfect plan and we're ready for our journeys in life. Unfortunately, our lives don't always go in the directions we intend. Many times storms come along unexpectedly and wash away those lovely creations we had prepared in our minds. We wake up one morning and find our perfect little pathways have suddenly become twisted and difficult to follow.

We need to remember the storms of our lives that pass in the night are simply temporary obstacles in our path. God has our life's pathway marked so clearly if we would only trust Him to lead us in the right direction. He is the Master Painter and He has drawn the most perfect "chalk walk" for us. All we have to do is follow it, even when an occasional rainstorm washes away the path. After the storm is over, He's right back on that sidewalk making more magnificent masterpieces for us to follow.

Challenge of the Day

How do you handle it when life's storms come along and wash away what you thought was the perfect pathway? Do you ask God to help you find another path that goes in the direction He so perfectly planned for you?

Day 17

Crown Of Life

"Do not be afraid of what you are about to suffer. I tell you, the devil will put some of you in prison to test you, and you will suffer persecution for ten days. Be faithful, even to the point of death, and I will give you the crown of life." ~Revelation 2:10

God does not exempt us from suffering. All of us face hardships in our daily lives. But He encourages us not to be afraid when we face life's challenges and He commands us to be faithful. He says to those who are faithful, *"I will give you the crown of life!"*

Wow! That's a lot to digest. Let's try dissecting this idea taken from Revelation.

Suffering: When we suffer, we often ask, "Why me, God?" But maybe the question should be, "Why **not** me?" Even though we never fully understand why we have to suffer, what makes us think we should be exempt from suffering? When we suffer, we are made stronger because our faith has been tested and we have survived it.

Fear: God encourages us not to be afraid. We should not allow difficult times to turn us away from Him. We will all be tested–even Jesus was tested. But He will walk beside us through the hills and valleys of life.

Faith: Totally trust God. When we experience any type of suffering in our lives, we must allow God to reassure our hearts and minds. Faith says that even though there are dark clouds overhead, we know the sun is still there. We need to let Him walk our life journey with us.

Crown of Life: And if we are faithful, God will reward us with the crown of life. In other words, God will have a reward waiting for us in heaven! What more could we ask?

We will never be able to comprehend why suffering occurs, but the one thing we know is this—God has the master plan. Let's ask God to walk beside us and give us the wisdom, guidance, and courage to help us when we are hurting. Keep the faith and trust in Him for our reward will be the crown of eternal life!

Challenge of the Day

When you face hardships, do you go to God to help get you through it? Can you recall a time when you were being tested? What was the result?

The E-World Diet

"Through Jesus, therefore, let us continually offer to God a sacrifice of praise—the fruit of lips that confess His name." ~Hebrews 13:15

Diets! Diets! Diets! Regardless of height, weight, or inches, most women have fretted over their weight at one time or another. And the world has certainly tried to come to our rescue. For example, we have Weight Watchers, Jenny Craig, Nutri-Systems and South Beach. But perhaps we should be focusing on a different kind of diet—an "E-World Diet."

What exactly is an "E-World Diet?" First, let's look at the amazing world of technology that surrounds us. We have Smart Phones, iPads, laptops, iPods, Kindles, just to name a few electronic "gadgets." Many of us are overwhelmed with cell phone calls, texts, e-mails, voice mails, calendars, Facebook, Twitter, FaceTime, and even on-line games. With all these incredible devices at our fingertips, it doesn't take long to realize we may be spending entirely too much time in the electronic world. Perhaps we need to go on an "E-World Diet!"

Even with all of these incredible inventions that have dazzled us over the past few years, it is important that we continue to keep

God as our top priority. We need to be just as diligent in keeping a daily connection to God as we are in checking our email every day. The only way we can learn what God has to say to us is through His word, not on Facebook! Even though the internet offers us a wealth of information, nothing is more important and can offer us more wisdom than God's instruction book and seeking His guidance through prayer.

Of course, our world of technology is a fantastic tool and offers unique avenues of communication. But how much more essential it is for us to be communicating with our heavenly Father. Somehow, we need to find a balance between our "E-World" and our spiritual world. Once we get our daily servings of God's word and find that "balanced diet," our hunger will be satisfied in a much more meaningful way. Could we ask for a better diet plan?

Challenge of the Day

How much time would you estimate you spend on some electronic "gadget" each day? Do you think you should be devoting some of that time to God? If so, how can you budget your time so you are communicating with Him as much or more than you are communicating in the E-World?

Day 19

Shoes: Walking In Obedience

"And this is love: that we walk in obedience to His commands...His command is that you walk in love."
~2 John 1:6

Many women have a real passion for shoes! Researchers say that people can "accurately judge 90 percent of a stranger's personality simply by looking at that person's shoes." The *Journal of Research in Personality* published a study that found "shoes serve as nonverbal cues with symbolic messages." Just for fun, let's look at the shoes we are wearing now and ask ourselves what those shoes reveal about our personalities. Now, here's what the "experts" have to say: "practical, sensible, or functional shoes are worn by agreeable people; ankle boots are often worn by people with more aggressive personalities; and more fashionable, trendy, or flashy footwear is typically worn by extroverts."

Do we agree with the "experts" and feel that our personalities fit the types of shoes we wear? Do we really believe that someone can look at our shoes and tell something about us as a person? Believe it or not, according to research, shoes do tend to reveal information about the owner's personality. Now, the next time we try on a pair of shoes, maybe we should consider what that pair of shoes says about us!

Now let's stop and ask ourselves, "Is God looking at our shoes to determine who we are, or is He looking at our hearts?" We know the answer to that question. God probably isn't too concerned if we are wearing a fashionable heel or a worn-out sneaker. But let's be assured that He is looking to see if our hearts are obedient, filled with love and service, or is it a heart that is wayward and defiant?

Our walk through life should not be determined by something as frivolous as a pair of shoes. More importantly, we need a deep-rooted relationship with God. We need Him walking right along with us. As we slide our feet into our shoes each day, let's make certain that God is filling our hearts and that we are "walking" in the shoes He has chosen for us!

Challenge of the Day

Are you more worried about your fashionable shoes or your heart for God? When others look at you, do they notice your shoes or your attitude of faith? Share how you are walking in obedience with God.

41

Refresh And Renew

"Create in me a pure heart, O God, and renew a steadfast spirit within me. Do not cast me from your presence or take your Holy Spirit from me. Restore to me the joy of your salvation and grant me a willing spirit, to sustain me." ~Psalm 51:10-12

As young adults, Jim and Rachel had always been devout Christians. Their relationship had even begun during a Community Impact Day when each of their separate churches was involved in a building project for a needy family. However, as their lives together continued down the usual path—marriage, careers, and eventually, children—they were simply not as involved in the church as they had been a few years back. Their lives were good, but Jim and Rachel both realized something was missing. And that something was God.

Everyday life can make it difficult to keep our attention on God. Our days can easily become "maxed out" with being busy. Maybe we're carpooling kids to various school functions or possibly caring for an elderly parent. Perhaps our jobs are demanding and stressful and leave little time for spiritual reflection. Unfortunately, this can cause our relationship with God to suffer; we simply do not make time to worship God as we should. Often, we tend to put Him on a back burner with a promise, "I'll get right back to you, God!" Of course, as the alarm goes off each morning, we know how quickly we forget that promise.

Fortunately, we have a loving and forgiving God. Scripture reminds us that we need to renew our spirit and replenish our faith. Does our own faith need to be refreshed and renewed? Let's ask ourselves two questions: How much time do we spend in God's word each day? How much time do we spend in prayer each day? If we are filled with doubt about these questions, then now might be a good time to re-establish our relationship with God.

How can we accomplish this? As difficult as it might be, we could get up a few minutes earlier and read a devotional as we drink our morning coffee, or we could get involved in a women's Bible study. Do whatever it takes to spend some time with God. When we take the time to refresh and renew our relationship with Him, it will bring us peace and joy like nothing else ever could!

Challenge of the Day

Do you find that your spiritual life has suffered because your daily routine is so hectic? When you look at your busy schedule, can you find a spot during the day when you could spend some time alone with God? When would be the best time for **you** to get your spirit renewed?

Best Policy: Honesty

"A false witness will not go unpunished, and he who pours out lies will not go free." ~Proverbs 19:5

"Oh, it was just a little white lie, Taylor. I'm not going to worry about it!" declared Stephanie. "But Stephanie, a lie is a lie and you just blatantly lied to your sister. Now you'll have to tell another lie to try to cover up this one when you explain it to your mom," Taylor exclaimed. "Don't you think telling her the truth would have been better for all of us in the long run? Sooner or later, the truth will come out!"

How sad it is that lying is such a common occurrence in today's society. Perhaps there are times when we even catch ourselves embellishing a story to make a better impression, exaggerating the truth to help a co-worker, or telling a "little white lie" to spare someone's feelings. And unfortunately, one lie usually leads to another lie in order to validate the story. Oh, what a tangled web we weave!

Surprisingly, a recent poll "indicated that 91 percent of us lie regularly. One in five can't get through a single day without telling a lie." (*Dennison Forum*) Aren't those staggering statistics? In Psalms 31:5, God is called the *God of Truth*, and our God of Truth desires that we convey the truth in all we do, all we say, and in all we think. He also admonishes us in Proverbs 12:22 that *"the Lord detests lying lips, but He delights in men who are truthful."*

Whenever we find ourselves in a web of dishonesty, whether it be one of our own creation or someone else's, we should recognize that we are disgracing the truth of the scripture. God thought honesty was so incredibly important that He made it one of the Ten Commandments, *"You shall not give false testimony against your neighbor."* [Exodus 20:16] If God commands that we be honest, both with ourselves and with others, how can we choose to tell those "little white lies"? Honesty will bring peace to our lives and will certainly make us shine in the eyes of our heavenly Father. There is definitely **truth** in that old adage, *"Honesty is the best policy!"*

Challenge of the Day

Can you remember a time when you blatantly lied? Do you lie often? If so, why do you feel the need to be dishonest?

The Treasure Hunt

"Do not store up for yourselves treasures on earth where moth and rust destroy, and where thieves break in and steal. But store up for yourselves treasures in heaven, where moth and rust do not destroy, and where thieves do not break in and steal. For where your treasure is, there will your heart be also." ~Matthew 6: 19-21

We've probably all seen one of those old movies about pirates burying their treasure. Often the valuables were buried in a treasure chest in some far-off land, and a treasure map was required to find the exact spot where the goodies were buried. Perhaps that's where the expression "X marks the spot" originated.

But we know that in reality, there is no pirate gold buried on some deserted island. What we have is a treasure far more precious than gold or jewels. Our treasure lies buried in our hearts because we have a God who has given us the gift of love, grace, and peace. What's more, He has left us a treasure map to follow. The map is God's word. In it, He has given us very clear instructions on how to discover life's most precious gifts. With scripture as our guide, we are bound to find God's greatest treasures.

How good are we at searching for God's treasure? If His "map" gives us specific directions, are we diligently seeking the bounty He has in store for us? Think about how wonderful the gifts are that God has so graciously bestowed on us. How much time do we spend seeking His will and studying His plan? He wants us to find His loving treasures and keep them safely buried in our hearts. Our treasures shouldn't be worldly "things;" those come and go with the passage of time. He wants us to put our most valuable "gifts" in the safest place of all...in His heart.

We should take some time each day to study God's "map." The X on His treasure map will bring us the most wonderful treasures we could ever imagine!

Challenge of the Day

Do you refer to God's "treasure map" daily? What do you think is the most precious treasure God has given you? Why?

"I Don't Live There Any Longer!"

"Therefore, if anyone is in Christ, he is a new creation; the old has gone, the new has come!" ~2 Corinthians 5:17

It was New Year's Eve and Bonnie was having a hard time joining in the celebration. As she took a few minutes to reflect over the past year, she was amazed at how much had happened in her life in just twelve short months. Some of her memories brought tears to her eyes as she recalled the anger and disappointment of a terrible loss. But Bonnie also smiled through her tears, remembering other events which had brought her such incredible joy. Yes, it had been a rough year but Bonnie knew that with the beginning of every year, she was given an opportunity for a fresh, new start.

Most of us have experienced a hurtful situation in the past, but a slogan that can help us overcome some negative baggage we may be carrying simply states, **"Don't judge me by my past. I don't live there any longer."** This little adage reminds us that none of us has to deal with a painful past because it's just not there anymore. God provides us the opportunity every day to start over and walk away from past hurts and regrets. Getting rid of the emotional baggage of our past allows us the freedom to move on and look forward to a positive future.

Praise God that our "old" life can pass away and a "new" life can begin! (paraphrased from 2 Corinthians 5:17) What a comforting feeling to know He gives us each day as a new beginning. Knowing that God is walking with us on our earthly journey brings a comfort and assurance money cannot buy!

Whether we have a heart filled with regret or a life filled with blessings, we need to praise God for the opportunity He gives us for a new beginning each day. Isn't it an awesome feeling to say, "What's done is done; I can let go of the painful past...**I don't live there any longer!"?**

Challenge of the Day

Is there an incident or situation from your past that causes you pain? What can you do to help yourself let go of the past and turn yourself around to face your future with hopeful anticipation?

Train Or Complain?

"I sought the Lord, and he answered me;
He delivered me from all of my fears." ~Psalm 34:4

All of us know people who seem to be successful at everything they do. They have positive attitudes and a strong work ethic—that's why they succeed. And we have all experienced people who are never satisfied with anything. They whine and are disgruntled no matter what the situation. What a vast difference between an uplifting attitude and an attitude that is always looking at what's wrong. Successful people train while unsuccessful people complain!

Are we training and pushing toward our goals **or** do we have plenty of good intentions but all we do is make excuses and complain? For example, think of an Olympic athlete. Can we imagine the years of training and the number of hours required to represent our country in the Olympics? Certainly these athletes don't waste any of their time and energy complaining about their demanding training routines. Are they afraid to move on to the next level of competition? Or do they recognize the importance of dedication and push themselves toward their ultimate goal? Imagine if Gold Medalist Gabby Douglas had complained about all the sacrifices and setbacks she experienced on her path to winning the gold! Instead, she gave all the credit to God!

While training is an important part of achieving our goals, we should try not to let the fear of failure keep us from reaching them. All of us make mistakes, but we can learn from them and, hopefully, do better next time. Just keep a positive attitude, ask for God's help, and never forget the importance of placing Him at the center of our journeys. We should let God be our personal coach and trainer and allow His word to be our game plan. With God on our team, there is no reason to complain...we'll always come out a winner!

Challenge of the Day

How do you see yourself—as a trainer or a complainer? What can you do to include God in your game plan?

IT!

"Do nothing out of selfish ambition or vain conceit, but in humility consider others better than yourselves." ~Philippians 2:3

We have all met someone who just thinks they are "IT!" Oh yes, they are arrogant, self-centered, and think the world revolves around them! And if we have any doubt they are "IT," all we have to do is ask them. They can set us straight in the blink of an eye. The "ITs" in this world know who they are and where they are going. Well, at least they think they do.

People who have "The 'IT' Syndrome" are often sad, lonely people. They have few real friends because they see themselves as better than everyone else. They convince themselves they're the ones who have "got it together" while we are the ones floundering around to find our way. We can almost pity a person who behaves and believes this way. Clearly, scripture teaches us that we are never to consider ourselves better than anyone else; we are to be humble.

Being humble doesn't mean we have to degrade our abilities or potential. It does mean we need to have an honest perspective of who we are and what our true purpose is in life. Are we here to serve ourselves, to win at any cost, to put ourselves above everyone else? Or are we meant to follow the example of Christ, humble ourselves and serve rather than be served. In 1 Peter 5:5-6, he writes, *"Clothe yourself with humility...because God opposes the proud but gives grace to the humble. Humble yourselves, therefore, under God's mighty hand, that He may lift you up in due time."*

When people describe us, don't we want them to use words like honest, respectful, thoughtful, caring, humble, a child of God? There's nothing wrong with being confident and self-assured because we know we have the Lord on our side and in our hearts. But there is no place for "The 'IT' Syndrome" in the heart of a true believer.

Challenge of the Day

When you are really good at something, do you have a hard time being humble about it? What do you see as the characteristics of a person who is truly humble?

Day 26

Let Your Conscience Be Your Guide

"But when He, the Spirit of truth, comes,
he will guide you into all truth." ~John 16:13

As little children, we usually went to our parents for advice when we had a tough choice or a difficult decision to make. A wise parent often left the choice up to the child, depending on the seriousness of the decision, by making this statement, "Think about both sides of the problem; then let your conscience be your guide." In this way, the parent was helping the child think through the situation and come up with her own solution. In the meantime, the parent prayed the child would make the right decision.

What does the word "conscience" actually mean? The most common definition of the word simply refers to our ability to know right from wrong and realize that doing the wrong thing will usually have consequences later. We should feel bad about it when we do wrong. Our conscience, actually the voice of the Holy Spirit, is that little "Jiminy Cricket" voice in our heads that says, "You always need to try to do what is right."

If we are completely truthful, there have probably been times when we have ignored old Jiminy Cricket and proceeded to do something we knew was wrong. Maybe it was due to peer pressure or it was just easier or "everybody else was doing it!" Perhaps it worked out well for a while, but going against our conscience will most likely lead to disastrous results.

Isn't it wonderful when we finally discover that the little Jiminy Cricket voice in our hearts is actually the voice of God? He is the one who has helped us distinguish right from wrong. He tries to give us that wise parental advice so we can make good choices and stay on the right path. We should make it a practice to listen to God's little warning voice. We need to follow our hearts and let His voice be our conscience and our guide!

Challenge of the Day

Has there ever been a time when you have done something that you knew was wrong but you went ahead and did it anyway? Why did you make that choice? What happened as a result of not following your conscience?

Day 27

Cold, Lukewarm, Or Hot?

*"O Lord, You have searched me and you know me. You know when I sit
and when I rise; You perceive my thoughts from afar. You discern my going
out and my lying down; You are familiar with all my ways."
~Psalm 139:1-3*

In recent years, being health conscious has become fashionable
in America. With so much emphasis placed on weight loss, the
phrase "everything in moderation" has certainly become
popular. It's as though anything is acceptable, as long as we do it
"in moderation." We can apply this phrase to just about any
aspect of our lives from eating and drinking, even to our faith.
We are sometimes afraid to be too hot or passionate about
displaying our love for the Lord because people might perceive
us to be overzealous. We certainly don't want to offend anyone.
Of course, we can't be cold in regards to religion; otherwise,
people might think we're nonbelievers. Therefore, we end up
"riding the fence" depending on our social circumstances. We
want our religion to be "comfortable." Most of us are lukewarm
at best.

Let's take a closer look at our spiritual thermometer. Is it cold,
lukewarm, or hot? Do we love God with all our minds, hearts,
and souls? Or do we love God when it's convenient or socially

acceptable? Do we display our faith "in moderation"? Or are we unafraid to let others know we are children of God?

Unfortunately, God doesn't like lukewarm. Read these words from Revelation 3:15-16: *"I know your deeds, that you are neither cold nor hot. I wish you were either one or the other! So, because you are* **lukewarm**—*neither hot nor cold—I am about to spit you out of my mouth!"* Those are very scary words straight from God. Maybe we'd better take another look at our spiritual thermometer and make certain we are not half-hearted Christians, that we are not practicing our faith "in moderation." Let's develop a heart for God that is on fire!!

Challenge of the Day

If you were to take your spiritual temperature today, would it read hot, cold, or lukewarm? What can you do to keep your gauge on hot?

Day 28

Acting 101

"Obey me, and I will be your God and you will be my people. Walk in all the ways I command you, that it may go well with you." ~Jeremiah 7:23

Staring into her tiny dorm room closet, Jenny couldn't decide what she wanted to wear tonight. She was headed for the usual campus hangout where she would meet up with a large group of friends. It was a fun place to go to celebrate the upcoming weekend and as with most social gatherings at school, it was important to **"see and be seen"**! As Jenny put on a trendy short skirt, a skimpy top and stylish high heels, she looked at herself in the mirror with a little twinge of guilt. She knew this provocative look was not really acceptable in God's eyes. But she had to play the part, to **"act cool"** in order to be accepted by the other students.

Jenny had a strong Christian upbringing, but being away at college and trying so hard to fit in made it difficult to hold on to those deep-rooted values. She kept those ideas tucked away in her heart because being a **good Christian girl** just wasn't a popular concept in the world of academia. It was difficult to be a positive role model for Christ, and it bothered her when she realized she was only **acting** as though she was enjoying herself at these parties.

These choices can be extremely challenging for all of us, young and old alike. We can easily find ourselves in social situations that are not conducive to our Christian values. What do we do in those situations? Do we participate and "act the part" just so we will fit in with the group? Or do we **act** on our knowledge of Christ and obey our conscience? The choice is ours, of course. We can choose to be a role model for the Lord, or we can simply "act out the role" that society dictates. God knows our hearts. Even if we are the greatest actresses in town, God knows our every thought. And He commands us to obey Him in all areas of our lives. There are no Academy Awards in heaven!

Challenge of the Day

Have you ever found yourself in a social situation where you felt guilty because you found it was necessary to "**act** the part"? Why did you feel that way?

Day 29

Patti Perfect

"His divine power has given us everything we need for life..." ~2 Peter 1:3

Patti sighed as she straightened up the files for what she felt was the hundredth time that day. "Why can't they do anything right?" she thought. And while Patti was going behind her co-workers' backs and doing things her way, they were thinking, "Every time I do something, Patti always finds something wrong with it. Why should I even bother?" Her co-workers had even nicknamed her "Patti Perfect."

Perfectionists are people who will accept nothing less than perfection, as the word implies. They usually set excessively high performance goals and are not satisfied unless everything meets those standards. And yes, they are often critical of themselves as well as others if those goals are not met.

Chances are, we all know a perfectionist, or maybe we are one ourselves! The sad thing about perfectionists is that they tend to feel frustration, aggravation, and even depression if the results of their efforts are not what they expect. For that reason, a true "Patti Perfect" has a hard time being a happy person because she just can't relax and enjoy even the simplest activity without stressing out about it. They miss the joy and satisfaction of an accomplishment because their expectations are too high and they're often disappointed with the results.

While being a high achiever is an excellent quality, God certainly has no intention of our being anywhere near perfection. He simply offers us grace and tells us in 2 Peter that *"His divine power has given us everything we need for life."* We need to do the best we can in all we do, and always ask for God's help when we have a difficult task. Remember, perfection doesn't need to be our ultimate goal. After all, Jesus is the only one who achieved true "perfection!"

Challenge of the Day

Have you ever known a "Patti Perfect"? If so, did you share with them about God and His divine power for their lives? Explain.

Day 30

Words, Words, Words

"A wise man's heart guides his mouth." ~Proverbs 16:23

How many words are there in the English language? Really, no one knows. Researchers estimate there are 988,968. Grammar teachers tell us that it's not necessarily the number of words we use that's important, it's how we craft our sentences: sentence structure, noun-verb agreement, dangling participles, prepositional phrases, and dependent and independent clauses. We all suffered through learning the proper rules of grammar in high school English class!

If God were here today, what do we think He would say about our **words**? Would He be concerned about how many words are in the dictionary or whether we used dangling participles in our sentences? Wouldn't He be more concerned about the words we choose when we are communicating with others? Interestingly enough, in school we were taught the rules of the English language, but did anyone ever teach a class in how we use our words?

Words can be dangerous things. They can be harmless or they can be devastating—it all depends on how we choose to use them. Plus, once we speak words or write words, those words can never be withdrawn. There is no magic delete button. Once we hit "send" or once we have verbalized our thoughts, we cannot take them back.

As Christians, we need to think before we speak or write. We need to let God filter our words through love and kindness, not hatred or anger. Our words should build up, not tear down. They should help, not hurt. If we use our words as positive testaments to God, we would never say anything we would be sorry for in the future. Don't allow anger or resentment to put words in our mouths that God would not want to hear. Let our words be a positive, shining light—even if our participles are dangling!

Challenge of the Day

Can you remember a time when **words** came out of your mouth that you were sorry for later? What were the consequences of speaking before you thought? Do you think before you speak now?

Day 31

Trust The Process

*"Now faith is being sure of what we hope for
and certain of what we do not see." ~Hebrews 11:1*

As Paula hung up the phone, her heart ached. She felt numb and helpless. Her divorce attorney had called to ask if she could stop by to sign the final papers. Even knowing for several months this day would eventually come, nothing could have prepared her for the feeling of devastating loss and finality that came with this phone call. All she could do now was cry and ask herself for the hundredth time, "What now? Where do I go from here? How can I live without Mark?" When we find ourselves in such overwhelming and emotionally complex situations, we often ask these kinds of questions. We simply can't believe that something so terrible could be happening to us.

Like Paula, we experience feelings of hopelessness and despair that can leave us bitter and angry. Those feelings can become so acute that many people attempt to fill the void left by their loss with substance abuse, promiscuity, or some other form of self-destructive behavior. But is this where we should turn to find healing for our wounded spirits?

Scripture tells us to have faith. Faith is the assurance that God is always there whether we are aware of it or not. He has the power to fill the void left by a broken heart. All we have to do is accept the fact that healing is a process. We may not find answers to our questions overnight; our hearts won't heal in a day. But as children of God, we need to trust Him, talk to Him, let Him know that we are trying to overcome our loss and that we can't do it without His help. We should ask Him to help us find the next path in our journey. We must have enough faith to know that He will take us through the whole healing process. As wise counsel once said, **"Trust the process…God is in control."**

Challenge of the Day

Has there ever been a time when you looked somewhere else for comfort after an emotional trauma? Were you finally able to look to God for help in setting yourself back on the right path? Describe the steps in your healing process.

Doing What Is Good

"Remind the people to be subject to rulers and authorities, to be obedient, to be ready to do whatever is good, to slander no one, to be peaceable and considerate, and to show true humility toward all men." ~Titus 3:1-2

Wow, that's quite a "To Do List"! Doing what is good can be quite a challenge for Christians. According to this scripture, we are told to be respectful, obedient, willing to serve, avoid gossip, do what is right, keep the peace, and be considerate. And on top of all that, we need to be humble about it! Is it possible for us to assume all of those qualities on a daily basis? Sounds like a pretty tall order for us, doesn't it? But as Christians, this is the kind of person we all should all be striving to be.

In Matthew 11:29, Jesus referred to himself as *"gentle and humble in heart."* Isn't our goal as Christians to be like Jesus? When we think about it honestly, do we consider ourselves gentle and humble **and** do we possess all of those other wonderful qualities mentioned above? If we were taking a "Doing What is Good" test based on this scripture, what kind of score would we make? Well, let's just try it! Take a minute and go through this list of Christ-like qualities and let's see how well we score on each one. We might find ourselves lacking in some and excelling in others. As we check off each attribute, we need to honestly evaluate ourselves and determine in which area we feel we might need some work. Now, think about how God can help us make a better score!

Today, as we go through our daily routines, let's stop and ask ourselves if we are passing the test. Are we serving, being obedient to God, keeping the peace, being considerate of others, and just how humble are we behaving today? By using this little test as a guide to being a better Christian, we can use Jesus as our role model and raise our "Doing What is Good" test scores to an A+!

Challenge of the Day

Tonight as you settle in for the evening, think about your "To Do List." What did you do today that was most challenging as it relates to the "Doing What is Good" test? What can you do to make an even better score tomorrow?

Day 33

GPS--God's Precious Spirit

"Never will I leave you; never will I forsake you."
~Hebrews 13:5

While driving a chartered bus in Chicago, the bus driver got completely lost. He frantically tried to get the GPS to assist him with his directions, but panicked because the GPS was not getting a clear signal. The bus was now under the railroad tracks and in between skyscrapers. Even though he had driven in Chicago many times, he was struggling to drive his passengers to their destination. The driver was definitely lost.

Many of us have often felt like this on our life's journey. We have set our goals and worked toward getting to our destination, but somewhere along the line, we get lost. Yes, we have all been there. We start out with the best of intentions, but somehow we end up wandering around on the wrong side of the tracks.

Life takes us on a journey during which we travel all kinds of roads. Occasionally we travel down into some low and dark places, sometimes up on high mountaintops, and certainly we experience many twists and turns in between. Isn't it interesting how we can find ourselves attempting to follow His directions, but often, we make a wrong turn and the human side of us wanders into rugged terrain which can lead to devastation or disaster?

Often, we just need to *"be still and know that I am God" [Psalm 46:10]*. God is our GPS! He will offer us His divine Holy Spirit, if we will just take time out of our hectic journeys to listen to His advice. Don't get stuck under the railroad tracks or between the tall skyscrapers, those obstacles that prevent us from receiving God's signal. Regardless of the route our GPS takes us, remember it is important to spend time communicating with God. During this time, we need to ask God to lead and guide us, to give us wisdom and direction. God tells us, *"I will not leave you or forsake you."* Ask God for his divine Holy Spirit. Let Him be your life's GPS!

Challenge of the Day

Where is your GPS taking you today? Are you living by GPS or are you choosing your own route? Explain.

The Blame Game

"The Lord gave and the Lord has taken away; may the name of the Lord be praised. In all this, Job did not sin by charging God with wrongdoing."
~Job 1:21-22

Yvette walked out of her office in anger and disbelief. She had devoted over 15 years to this company, but because of the economy, the CEO had announced today they were downsizing. According to him, Friday would be her last day. As Yvette stormed out of the office, she couldn't believe this was really happening. She was devastated!

We have all had times in our lives when we have experienced a terrible loss of some kind. Our losses come in many forms— some of us have lost jobs, spouses, homes, money, health, and even loved ones. When we can't accept what has happened to us, we often tend to blame others for our situation. We don't want to face the fact that usually a tragic loss occurs as a result of something over which we have no control. But we feel as though we have to blame someone for our tragedy; it couldn't be our fault, right? Unfortunately, people often want to place blame on God. Some might think, "If He loved me, He would not take this from me!"

Can we honestly believe that God would purposely cause us to lose something that means so much? Look again at God's word and see how Job reacted to his incredible suffering. Job tore his robe off, shaved his head, and then fell to the ground in worship. He said, *"The Lord gave and the Lord has taken away; may the name of the Lord be praised."* Then it continues, *"In all of this, Job did not sin by charging God with wrongdoing."* In other words, Job didn't blame God. And we should not blame God either.

Scripture tells us over and over that we have a loving God who desires for us to be faithful and obedient to Him. When we experience a terrible loss in our lives, just look at Job. If anyone had a reason to play the blame game, it was certainly him. But he praised God because he had amazing faith in God's grace! Do we?

Challenge of the Day

Describe a time in your life when you experienced a great feeling of loss. Did you blame God or were you able to accept the fact that you had no control over your circumstances? Explain.

Day 35

Would The Real You Please Stand Up!

"Flee the evil desires of youth, and pursue righteousness, faith, love and peace, along with those who call on the Lord out of a pure heart."
~2 Timothy 2:22

As we look back on our lives, we have all been through many changes. We have gone from childhood, through the pain of adolescence, maybe college and then a career. Throughout all those stages of life, we have played many roles, but there has always been a strong desire for us to find our own niche. Sometimes we want so much to be liked and to be a part of a certain group that we sacrifice who we really are in order to "fit in." God created us to be social beings and, of course, we need to feel accepted and well liked in our circle of friends. However, there must be a point at which we look at our "friends" and ask ourselves, "Is this really me? Can I truly be myself when I am with this friend or this group, or do I feel like I have to change something about myself in order to please that person?"

If we look at ourselves honestly and answer that question with a yes, then there is something definitely wrong with that relationship. Of course, there are times when we have to adapt our behavior because of certain circumstances such as a business or professional setting. However, we should be able to relax and be ourselves among friends and know they accept us unconditionally. In trying to be a chameleon and change our personalities just to fit in with every group we encounter, we can easily lose sight of who we really are!

And why might this become a problem? We can try so hard to please the people around us that we lose sight of who we really should be trying to please—and that is God. The Lord knows us. He knows our hearts and our thoughts, and He is not happy with us when we try so hard to be someone other than who He created us to be. Instead of trying to impress and please our friends and acquaintances, we need to stop and think, "Is what I'm saying or doing pleasing to these people, or is it pleasing to God?" He's the one who knows the real person inside our hearts, and that is the one He truly loves!

Challenge of the Day

Have you ever been in a social situation when you felt like you had to act a certain way just to "fit in"? How did that make you feel? Are you sure the people you socialize with are not causing you to sacrifice who you really are and taking you away from your heavenly Father?

"I Can't!"

"Jesus looked at them and said, 'With man this is impossible, but not with God; all things are possible with God.'"
~Mark 10:27

Oh, how often we find ourselves saying, **"I can't!"** We've all had our share of experiences when we have said that four-letter word—"can't!" For some of us, those words could most definitely be referring to things like sewing, gourmet cooking, or doing some intricate craft project. Those just are NOT on our list of God-given talents. But the truth is, we actually *could* do all of those things. Sure, the results might not be up to Martha Stewart standards, and we may not be destined to be on Top Chef, but we **can** produce results. All we need is a sincere desire and a willingness to try. Many times, however, *our can'ts* aren't as simple as sewing or cooking. Have you ever heard these excuses made by people who frequently have the **"I can't"** mentality? They might sound something like this:

- **I can't** go on that mission trip. I could never travel to a third world country.
- **I can't** give my testimony, not in front of all of those people!
- **I can't** host a small group Bible Study. My house just isn't large enough.

- **I can't** work on my church's Community Impact Day. I've got a bad back.
- **I can't** share with those ladies. Someone else could do a better job than me.

Or maybe we've even heard ourselves say something along those lines. When it comes to serving our heavenly Father, do we sometimes find excuses that bring out those words, "**I can't!**"? The Bible tells us in Mark, *"All things are possible with God."* When we find ourselves wanting to serve Him in some capacity but don't because we see our own limitations, do we automatically think we **can't**? If so, perhaps we need to take a leap of faith. Consider what a difference just one person can make. What kind of impact could we have by taking one little step out of our comfort zones? We could possibly impact not just one life, but many, many lives. Isn't it worth the chance?

We serve a **big** God! He knows our hearts as well as our limitations. If He is walking with us as we choose a new path, we are capable of anything. There should be no doubt that God has the power to turn our "**I can'ts**" into "**I cans**"!

Challenge of the Day

Have there been times when you have said, "I can't" when you really could have done what was asked of you? Why do you think you avoid situations where you are called upon to serve but you have chosen to say "I can't" rather than "I will"?

Blueprint For Life

"But you, keep your head in all situations, endure hardship, do the work of an evangelist..." ~2 Timothy 4:5

The apostle Paul was facing imminent death when he wrote his letters to Timothy. His message expressed deep love and compassion, but they also conveyed Paul's overwhelming concern for the future of Christianity. He was passing on to Timothy the powerful teachings of Christ. Paul shared with Timothy the qualities necessary to be a faithful servant and minister, how to be disciplined and ready to endure trials and tribulations, and challenged him to hold tightly to the truth of God. He was giving Timothy the tools necessary to further God's Kingdom. In other words, Paul was mapping out for him a **blueprint for life.**

Paul's blueprint shows us that he was a person of deep faith, filled with hope and love, and that he possessed amazing insight. He stood courageously for truth and was empowered by the Holy Spirit. He understood the nature of God's love and the teachings of Jesus were deeply ingrained in every aspect of his life. He knew the true meaning of the blueprint.

No professional architect would dream of beginning a large project without a detailed blueprint to serve as a map for the construction of a building. It is carefully planned and contains every minute detail of the construction and every aspect of the structure. However, are we not God's greatest project? And isn't His word the perfect blueprint, provided by Him to show us how to live every aspect of our lives?

When we follow God's blueprint for life, we are given the strength to endure any hardship, to stay focused even in difficult situations, and to have faith enough to share God's word with others. God is the divine architect and we are His most magnificent masterpiece!

Challenge of the Day

Analyze your own blueprint for life. Does it follow the teachings of Paul? Is your life a shining example of Christ's love to others?

Day 38

The Mini Marathon

"Let us throw off everything that hinders and the sin that so easily entangles, and let us run with perseverance the race marked out for us."
~Hebrew 12:1

Lynn took a deep breath as she pinned her number on her race bib and reviewed the course map one last time. Finally, this was the big day, her first mini marathon. Never in her wildest dreams did she think she would be capable of running such a distance at her age; however, during the past year, Lynn had trained extensively. She thoroughly researched the preparation needed to run a successful race. She had persevered and knew she was ready to cross that finish line. Lynn read about running shoes, nutrition, hydration, training schedules, self-discipline, stretching, wristwatches, skin protection, and possibly most important, will power and the determination to succeed.

As Christians, our race to the finish line is very similar to that of a marathon runner. When we research (read the Bible), we learn about all of the elements necessary for us to reach our goal: salvation, grace, faith, love, hope, compassion, trust, obedience, forgiveness, serving, and gratitude, just to name a few. But we also learn that, as in running, determination and will power are essential attributes that will help us reach our ultimate goal—our "finish line" which is eternity in heaven.

The track is clearly marked for us. God has not promised the race will be an easy one. But with the right preparation and perseverance, we must run that marathon here on earth if we want to spend eternity with Jesus. Just imagine what it will be like when we finally cross that finish line and God greets us with, *"Well done, my good and faithful servant."* [Matthew 25:21] Persevere, dear friend!

Challenge of the Day

Have you reviewed your course map lately? Are you running on track, or do you need to make some changes in your course? If so, what changes do you think should be made?

Why, God, Why?

"God is our refuge and strength,
an ever-present help in trouble."
~Psalm 46:1

Deborah and Jessie were definitely the typical American family living the "American Dream." They both worked hard, had two great kids, a nice house, and shared lots of love with friends and family. But today, all of that was about to change. The oncologist was giving Jessie the results of his last PET Scan and it was bad news. The cancer had spread and there was very little they could do about it. It was just a matter of time. Leaving the doctor's office, Deborah broke into tears and cried all the way home. She kept praying, begging God for help. "God, I can't live without Jessie! Please, please, do something for him!" And then she cried out, "Why, God, oh why us?"

When we find ourselves in such devastating experiences—a bad diagnosis or some other catastrophic event—we often plead with God and beg Him to help us. We have a difficult time understanding the "why" of such terrible news. And sometimes, we even find ourselves becoming angry with God because we can't believe He would let something so terrible happen to us.

It's easy to let our faith get shaken in difficult times. We wonder what kind of plan God could possibly have that could justify our loss. However, this is exactly the time when our faith should become stronger to help us get through the tragedies we suffer. All we have to do is turn to God and instead of asking "Why me, God?", ask God to give us the strength and courage we will need to face the future. We have to trust God and try to understand that even though terrible things happen to us, He is always there to give us comfort and the courage we need to move forward. 1 Peter 5:6 assures us that if we *"humble ourselves, therefore, under God's mighty hand, that He may lift you up in due time. Cast all your anxiety on Him because He cares for you."* Trust in Him and He will eventually answer the question, "Why?"

Challenge of the Day

Has there ever been a time in your life when you have been angry with God and wondered **why** He allowed some tragedy to occur? How did you work through your anger? What did you learn from that experience?

Interruptions

"I tell you, get up, take your mat and go home. He got up, took his mat and walked out in full view of them all. This amazed everyone and they praised God, saying, 'We have never seen anything like this!'"
~Mark 2:11-12

As Brittany was driving to work, she was singing and swaying to the music on the radio when suddenly, that nerve-shattering noise jolted her right in the middle of her song. "BUUZZZZ! BUUZZZZ! BUUZZZZ! This is a test of the Emergency Broadcast System," the announcer declared. Immediately, Brittany threw her head back and rolled her eyes and shouted at the radio, "Are you kidding me? That was my favorite song you just ruined!" Brittany's happy mood was completely destroyed because of that ugly interruption!

Of course, having something as trivial as our favorite song on the radio interrupted is nothing too devastating. But there are instances when interruptions can be quite disturbing. The Bible gives us several examples of Jesus getting interrupted during His ministry. Let's look at one example: in Mark, we are told that Jesus was teaching to a room full of people. A group of men had heard of Jesus' miraculous healing powers and wanted desperately to present their paralytic friend to Him. However, there was such a large crowd, they could not get their friend anywhere near Jesus, so while He was speaking, they cut a hole in the roof and lowered the man down in front of Jesus. Needless to say, they interrupted Jesus in the midst of His lesson and He could have easily gotten upset because of the disturbance. But of course, Jesus immediately understood the situation and healed the man because of his great faith as well as the faith of his friends. Once the man was healed, the people who witnessed the miracle were astonished and realized that Jesus was truly the Son of God.

Instead of being annoyed or simply dismissing this man, Jesus used this interruption as an opportunity to do something wonderful and perform a miracle. When we get interrupted in our daily routines, do we lash out in anger or irritation? Or do we take that interruption as a time to stop and catch our breaths, possibly use that time to do something good for someone else? The next time we are interrupted, let's use it as a God moment. Think of it as a "divine pause," a chance to be an example of God's patience and love!

Challenge of the Day

Do you remember a time when you allowed some interruption to make you angry? How did you react? How might you respond differently in the future?

Day 41

My Rock And My Salvation

"He alone is my rock and my salvation; he is my fortress, I will never be shaken." ~Psalm 62:2

Marci had moved back to her hometown to help take care of her aging parents, but she had no idea how difficult this was going to be. First came the financial burden of the nursing home followed by an overwhelming feeling of guilt. She found herself on such an emotional rollercoaster that she gave in to the despair and apparent hopelessness of her situation. She found herself in such a state of depression, she wondered how she could ever possibly get herself back to normal. Marci had definitely fallen into a pit from which there was no obvious escape.

Then, one day over coffee with an old friend, she confided she was at her wit's end. Her friend suggested to Marci she needed to put her hope in God. She explained that God is our rock and during these tough times, when we find ourselves on shaky ground, we have only to turn to God and ask for His help. Eventually, her friend led Marci to a Christian counselor who, through scriptural guidance, gave her hope and direction.

How many times in our lives do we feel as though we have fallen head first into a pit of despair and hopelessness? We get to the point where we feel there is no way out and we give up. Try as we might, we just can't seem to find a sturdy rock that will provide a strong foothold to help us climb up and out of that pit.

When we find ourselves in a dark place, perhaps it would be helpful to re-assess our situation. We should not be ashamed if we find ourselves needing additional direction. It is never too late to speak with a professional, possibly a pastor or counselor. But remember, God is there in the pits with us as well as those high places of joy. All we have to do is reach out for His strong, loving hand, and He can bring us out of the darkness into His eternal light. He is our strength and our rock!

Challenge of the Day

Describe a time when you experienced a difficult situation. Did you lean on God for understanding and direction? What advice would you suggest to a friend like Marci?

In God's Eyes

"For we are God's workmanship, created in Christ Jesus to do good works, which God prepared in advance for us to do." ~Ephesians 2:10

The twins were at the age when they had to ask a million questions. During a large family reunion, they cornered their Aunt Frances and asked her repeatedly, "Who is that?" Aunt Francis patiently looked around the crowded room and began her introduction of each family member.

From a distance, Jody listened as Aunt Frances carefully described several of the family guests: "Now, that's Uncle Bob...he's a veterinarian...you know, a doctor who takes care of animals...where you would take Pluto if he got sick. He's a really nice man!"

"Oh, and that is your mom's cousin, Krista. She's in college right now studying to be an engineer. No, not the kind that drives a train...the kind that builds bridges you will drive across someday. Krista is really sweet and very, very smart."

As Jody listened intently to each person's description, she began to wonder just how Aunt Frances might describe her. "Oh, Jody is *just* a stay-at-home mom taking care of you two angels," she might say. "She doesn't really do a whole lot." For a moment,

Jody felt a twinge of guilt and wondered if she had made the right decision about leaving her successful career to stay at home with her children.

Then Jody smiled as she remembered how she had turned to God for His help in her decision. It had been a difficult one to make, but she realized God had a plan for her. Prior to making her choice, she and her husband had committed the decision to prayer. God gently reminded her that during this season of her life, she needed to focus on being the best mother she could possibly be to those two babies.

Isn't it great that God doesn't compare us to others? He has made each of us unique. God doesn't have to ask, "Who is that?" He knows us better than we know ourselves. **Through His eyes**, we are all His children, beautifully and wonderfully made!

Challenge of the Day

How would Aunt Frances have described you? Are you pleased with the attributes you possess? If you are, describe your positive qualities. If you're not pleased, then how can you change your opinion?

Day 43

Take Your Time

"My dear brothers, take note of this: Everyone should be quick to listen, slow to speak, and slow to become angry." ~James 1:19

Leigh Ann stood teary eyed as she listened to April, her colleague, shouting at her. Day after day, April whined and complained about her family, co-workers, supervisors, and life in general. While Leigh Ann knew she didn't deserve the harsh tones and criticism, she realized April was simply taking her frustrations and discontent out on her. Sometimes people scream loudest at those they love most. Trying hard to be understanding, Leigh Ann recognized the pain her friend was suffering and showed as much grace as she could.

In scripture, James urges us to be *"quick to listen, slow to speak, and slow to become angry."* Oh, how we all need to heed this advice! Many of us wear our hearts on our sleeves and too often our emotions take over and we say or do things we shouldn't. But when we're in the middle of a heated conversation, isn't it difficult to show grace? Our natural response is usually to become defensive, to strike back at our verbal attacker, and we get angry because we believe we are being treated unfairly. We want our opinions and ideas to be heard.

We all tend to think our opinions are the most important, but what if our opinions hurt others? Do words spoken in thoughtless anger really help anyone? Honestly, most of us talk too much, listen too little, and many times we become angry too quickly. Next time we find ourselves in a situation similar to Leigh Ann's, remember James' advice: (1) think before we speak; (2) listen to what the other person is really saying and try to understand **why** they are lashing out at us; and (3) remember that fighting back, returning anger for anger, is not the way God wants us to deal with confrontation. He would want us to take a step back, take a deep breath, and **take our time** when we are sharing His grace.

Challenge of the Day

Do you remember a time when you spoke without thinking **or** didn't listen enough **or** angered too quickly? What happened as a result of your actions? What will you do differently next time?

Day 44

A Grandmother's Prayer

"I will instruct you and teach you in the way you should go; I will counsel you and watch over you." ~Psalm 32:8

Having grandchildren is such a blessing and something many women eagerly anticipate. When Jeanine's first grandbaby came along, being "Nana" was a little more difficult than she thought it would be. When little Claire was born with colic, Jeanine knew her daughter and son-in-law needed a break from the constant heart-wrenching screams, tears, bouncing, and walking the floor. She volunteered to keep Claire one day a week just to give Claire's mom and dad a little time to recuperate and regenerate before the next round of colicky screaming.

One day during a rare quiet moment, Jeanine was bouncing tiny Claire on her knee. Her Bible was on the table nearby and she opened it randomly to Psalm 32:8 where she read, *"I will instruct you and teach you in the way you should go; I will counsel you and watch over you."* Oh, how Jeanine's heart grew warm; this was exactly what she wanted to do for this precious baby. She immediately drew Claire close and read the verse out loud. She said softly, "Claire, this is going to be **your** verse!" Each week, Jeanine would read this scripture to Claire. What more could a grandmother want than for God to be first and foremost in her grandchild's life?

Jesus loved children and knew how important it was to teach them about God. In Matthew, He said, *"Let the little children come to me, and do not hinder them, for the kingdom of heaven belongs to such as these."* [Matthew 19:14] As our children grow up, they are influenced by so many non-Christian examples. Their innocence is gradually depleted as they are exposed to things our society says are acceptable today. But as a parent, it is our responsibility to instruct our children in the ways associated with God's word. Let's pray for God's guidance in bringing up our babies to walk the right paths. Let that be the legacy we leave for our grandchildren. What prayer could be more important than this one coming straight from a grandmother's heart?

Challenge of the Day

When was the last time you prayed for a child? Why do you think it is so valuable for our children to know and serve God?

Day 45

The Game Of Life

"Give thanks to the Lord, for He is good;
His love endures forever." ~Psalm 118:1

M any of us loved to play board games when we were kids. Countless hours were spent enjoying those classic games like Sorry, Candyland, Chutes and Ladders, and Monopoly. And what made those games so much fun was the anticipation of what was going to happen to the little token as it hopped its way around the board, completely at the mercy of the roll of the dice. Sometimes that little token would land in a good space—one that meant either winning something extra, getting another turn, or a bonus spin. Unfortunately, sometimes it landed in a bad space which meant some sort of penalty, losing a turn, having to go back to square one, or ending up in jail without passing go or collecting $200.

If we think about it, there are times when our lives feel as if we're one of those little tokens, moving around the game board of our lives. We move along, space by space, never knowing what will come with the next roll of the dice. But it's comforting to think that God is the one playing the game, and He is carefully moving us around that board, guiding our steps and knowing exactly where we're going to land. He can see the whole picture while we can only see the space right in front of us. If we look back at our lives, can't we clearly see God's hand steering us in the direction He wants our lives to go, even when we cannot?

Where do we see ourselves on our own life's game board? Are we in a good space right now? If we are, praise God, because He has guided us and blessed our lives in so many ways! Or maybe we find ourselves in a bad space. If we do, praise God, because He has promised us that He will always be there for us. We can be assured that **"this too shall pass."** We just need faith that God's love will get us through the bad spaces in life. With His help, we will always come out a winner in **the game of life**!

Challenge of the Day

Did you enjoy playing board games as a child? Perhaps you still do! If you could think of a board game that best describes your life right now, what would it be and why?

Day 46

"Keeping Up With The Joneses"

"The Lord is my shepherd, I shall not want." ~Psalm 23:1

W e've all heard the old cliché, "keeping up with the Joneses!" And of course, we all understand just what that implies. Society places such tremendous importance on wealth and materialism. Many people feel the more "things" they possess, the higher their social position will climb. Unfortunately, we don't know who "the Joneses'" really are, but for some reason, they have become the benchmark by which our social status is based. As a result of this societal pressure for more possessions, many people make decisions regarding purchases of houses, cars, electronics, and even clothing, based on what their friends and neighbors have. These decisions often lead to widespread debt and even bankruptcy.

Simple question: How rich do we want to be? When we answer that question, do we answer in terms of dollars and cents? That would be the logical answer in regard to wealth as the world sees it. Or when asked the same question as a Christian, do we use a much different frame of reference than "the Joneses"? Hopefully, our first thought is how rich we are in the "things" God wants for us. He has given us a wonderful definition of the word "**rich**."

Some of the richest people in the world are those who have meager budgets and small investment portfolios, but they are **rich** in Christ. Richness in Jesus Christ and His word brings treasures that money cannot buy. The Holy Spirit produces a sense of peace and joy that has no price tag—it's free!

In Galatians 5:22-23, we are taught the fruits of the spirit: love, joy, peace, patience, kindness, goodness, faithfulness, gentleness, and self-control. These are the possessions that God has willed for us. If we are rich in those spiritual gifts, how can we believe that "keeping up with the Joneses" will give us the ultimate joy? Instead of worrying about the Joneses of this world, let's try harder to keep up with **God**!

Challenge of the Day

Have you ever caught yourself trying to "keep up with the Joneses?" Assess your spiritual wealth. Do you need to make a deposit in your spiritual bank? If so, how would you do it?

Day 47

W*A*1*T

"Be still, and know that I am God." ~Psalm 46:10

Webster's Dictionary's definition of **wait** is "to remain stationary in readiness or expectation." In this "hurry-up, I want everything now world," it is often difficult for us to wait. Very few of us want to remain stationary, to just sit around and wait for life to happen. It seems in all aspects of our lives, we want what we want and we want it **now**! Besides, waiting can be so aggravating: waiting in a long line, waiting at a stop light that seems to last forever, or waiting on someone who is late to arrive. Many of us just have a hard time with waiting!

Often, we pray about the desires of our hearts, but then we find it difficult to wait for God's answer. When God does finally respond to our prayers, His answer might not be what we are expecting at all. Perhaps He directs us down a totally different path, and we are left scratching our heads, questioning His reasoning.

God has promised to hear his children when we pray, but it's up to us to *"be still and know that He is God."* We have to be willing to stop, to be stationary, so we can hear what God has to say to us. Even if He doesn't respond according to our wishes or in the timely manner we desire, we must realize that God knows best. We have to trust and have faith enough to wait for God's plan to unfold for us.

We need to pray diligently and remain stationary until our hearts feel we have heard from God. Be patient and wait for God because He will hear our prayers and answer them in His own time. Just as we do when our own children listen, obey, believe, and excel, God will smile down on us for trusting Him and having the patience to listen. Try to remember that He has our best interests at heart; we need to recognize the direction God wants us to travel. As Jeremiah explains, *God knows the plans He has for us* (paraphrased from Jeremiah 29:11). Just **wait**!

Challenge of the Day

Has there ever been a situation in your life when you have prayed about something and then hurried, trying to handle it on your own? Describe it. How would the results have been different if you had waited and let God work things out for you?

A Family Tradition

"Train a child in the way he should go, and when he is old
he will not turn from it." ~Proverbs 22:6

Over the years, Margaret's family had created a wonderful
Thanksgiving tradition. She put each family member's
name into a beautiful crystal bowl, and after dinner,
Margaret's husband would draw one person's name. Then, that
lucky family member would share what he/she had been
thankful for during the past year. Many times these were stories
of successes, some large, some small. But sometimes, they would
relate struggles they had encountered and share the life lesson
that had been learned as a result. After recalling these meaningful
events, that person would draw the next person's name out of
the bowl and it was then their turn to share their own
Thanksgiving stories. After all the children and grandchildren
were finished, Margaret and her husband would share their
thankfulness.

A tradition such as this can be a great opportunity for family
members to communicate with each other and gain a better
understanding of each other's feelings. With much laughter and
even a few tears, Margaret's heart overflowed with joy as she
listened to her children give God the glory for their
accomplishments. They also shared how they leaned on Him

when struggles arose. In both cases, whether success or struggle, all of Margaret's children knew their lives were in God's hands. What a blessing to know her children had such strong faith and had grown into these remarkable young Christians!

As a parent, one of our most important responsibilities is to raise children who are grounded in faith. We should serve as role models for them and teach them to follow God's teachings. What better testimony to our Christian legacy than to have children who carry on our tradition of love and faith in Christ!

Challenge of the Day

Have you spoken with your family members lately about their accomplishments and their struggles? Have you encouraged them to lean on God for understanding and guidance?

Are You A Martha?

"But Martha was distracted by all the preparations that had to be made. She came to Him and asked, 'Lord, don't you care that my sister has left me to do the work by myself? Tell her to help me!'" ~Luke 10:40

Siblings can be so different! Many times the oldest sibling likes to be the one in control, and this was definitely true of Martha, the older sister of Mary and Lazarus. Martha was hospitable and was probably thrilled that Jesus was a dinner guest in her home. No doubt, she enjoyed entertaining as many of us do. We might ask, "What's wrong with that?" Actually, there's nothing wrong with showing hospitality, but Martha was so concerned about pleasing, serving, and making everything perfect, she couldn't relax and enjoy her guests. And, as often happens with little sisters, Mary wasn't helping out in the kitchen and left Martha to do all the work. Mary was more interested in spending time with the guests than fussing over the meal. Eventually, Martha's frustrations lead to her outburst of anger against Mary.

How many times have we felt like Martha and in our frustration turned to God and said, "Dear God, this just isn't fair! Why should I be the one to do all the work or carry this responsibility?" But in Luke, Jesus gently adjusted Martha's attitude. He showed her that even though her gestures of preparation were thoughtful, they were not necessary. Yes, the meal was probably going to be wonderful, but it shouldn't have been her priority. He suggested she pay attention to what was more important—instead of worrying about being the perfect hostess, maybe she should have been a little more like Mary.

If we are blessed with brothers or sisters, we can sometimes let petty situations cause friction between us. When this happens, don't let disagreements or feelings of frustration lead to anger, bitterness or resentment. As Jesus explained to Martha, we need to get our priorities straight and nothing should be more important than showing love and patience to a precious sibling. We don't need to be a Martha and let anxiety or jealousy come between us and our relatives or friends. Be a Mary and enjoy the time we have to spend with the people who are the most precious to us!

Challenge of the Day

Have you ever had problems with a sibling over something that really wasn't that important? Have you let a petty disagreement affect your relationship with a loved one? Are you a Martha or a Mary?

God's Masterpiece

"For we are God's workmanship, created in Christ Jesus to do good works, which God prepared in advance for us to do." ~Ephesians 2:10

The Bible tells us that we are created in God's image. We are God's masterpiece! However, do we find that we are just too busy to pay attention to our Creator? Often, we get caught up in our daily routines and find that we just can't veer from those hectic schedules. Our days tend to revolve around our careers, our family obligations, household chores, communicating with friends and colleagues, not to mention sleeping, eating, and shopping; and every day we repeat this monotonous cycle. In addition, if we have school-aged children, throw in everything from soccer games and band practices to dance lessons and Cub Scout meetings. Life is busy!

When do we find time to fit God into our agendas? Interestingly enough, our relationship with God is somewhat of a love story; it is nothing short of a miracle that God loves us so much. Shouldn't we be willing to show that love right back to Him? If we honestly consider how much God has blessed us, how can we forget to include Him in our daily schedules? However, with the "busyness" of each day, our ambitions, dreams, and aspirations can consume us to the point that life becomes harried, hectic, and overwhelming. We can easily lose sight of the One who made us, the One who is most important. Maybe it's time we step back and look at the big picture. Are we trying hard to be the person God wants us to be? Are we committed to Him? What about God's desire for us to serve others? What kind of impact are we having on the lives of others?

God wants to be a part of our lives, to have a relationship with us. We are His magnificent creation and we need to allow God to guide our lives. Can we ever be worthy of His love? No, but we can certainly make Him a part of what we do every day. If we could ever realize what an incredible miracle we are, then we would be sure to find a place for God in the hustle and bustle of everyday life. We should turn our daily routine into something that God would consider a masterpiece of His love!

Challenge of the Day

Are you carving out time in your busy day to spend with God? Think about how many ways God has blessed your life. Don't you think you could find a way to say thank you for those blessings? How do you find a way to thank Him?

Day 51

The Beach

"When tempted, no one should say, 'God is tempting me.' For God cannot be tempted by evil, nor does He tempt anyone; but each one is tempted when, by his own evil desire, he is dragged away and enticed." ~James 1:13-14

There's just something about being at the beach...the sun on our faces, the salty air, the sand between our toes, and the breeze that cools us as we listen to the constant pounding of the surf. Occasionally, however, a terrible tragedy occurs at the beach, and it involves something called a riptide. On the surface, the water looks beautiful, even inviting. "Come on in for a little swim," it calls. We walk to the edge of the breaking waves and think, "I'll just get my toes wet. The water is so nice and warm and it feels good." So we wade in, maybe going just up to our ankles. We feel the sand wash out from under our feet as the waves recede and we decide there probably wouldn't be any harm in going out just a bit further. The water is clear, warm, and comforting as we venture out up to our knees and then up to our waists. "I can handle it," we think to ourselves when suddenly an unexpected wave overcomes us and we are swept off our feet. We lose our firm footing and the sand disappears from under us. That's when we feel the incredible force of the riptide beneath us. It tries to pull us under, forcing us to go deeper than we ever intended. We panic as our heads go under the water and we realize we are in trouble; we've lost control. As we fight our way to the surface, gasping for air and choking on the salty water, we suddenly feel two strong arms, the arms of Jesus, reaching down for us, pulling us back toward the shore.

Jesus is our lifeguard. How many times have we felt like we were drowning in a sea of sin, being pulled under by the evil one, but our Savior is always there to pull us back to safety. Whenever we feel like we are losing control, giving in to temptation, and being pulled away from our "rock," we need to reach out for those loving arms of Christ and allow Him to restore our faith.

Yes, the beach is a fantastic place and the sea is a beautiful and mysterious thing. But be mindful that just below the surface of those peaceful waters, a treacherous riptide can be waiting to pull us under. Let's allow Jesus to be our lifeguard as we wade in the waters of life.

Challenge of the Day

Have you ever felt as if you were being pulled under, giving into a temptation you knew was wrong, but you did it anyway? Describe the situation and how you overcame it with God's help.

Day 52

"I Do"

"Make vows to the Lord your God, and keep them."
~Psalm 76:11

When couples say "I Do," they make a commitment, a promise, a pledge, a vow. In a traditional ceremony, a man and woman promise to love each other for better or worse, in sickness and in health, for richer, for poorer, for the rest of their lives. And they are admonished to be faithful to each other, forsaking all others, dedicating their lives to each other's happiness and well-being.

If we have a relationship with God, we most likely remember the moment when we made the commitment and took the vow to accept Him into our lives. Did we promise to follow Him through the good and the bad, to be faithful to Him no matter what? Or have we drifted apart from God, gotten angry with Him because things just didn't work out the way we expected? Do we find ourselves using bitter words with Him such as, "God, I always get treated like this!" or "God, why me? You never let things work out the way I want them!" Have we forgotten the vows we made with God when we first promised to love and honor Him?

In our relationships with God, commitment continues to be the most important factor in our connection with Him just as with our spouses or significant others. Without a committed relationship, the "I Do" becomes meaningless and we develop a separation from God. However just as in a marriage, commitment takes work, work, and more work. It's something we must devote ourselves to every single day. Our commitment to God is the most important relationship in our lives. If we feel ourselves slipping away from God, let's decide today to renew our vows with Him. We need to refresh that pledge we made in our hearts when we accepted Him as our partner for life. Say, **"I do"** to God!

Challenge of the Day

What can you do to strengthen your commitment to God? What would it take for you to renew your vows to Him?

Choose To Lose

"I can do everything through Him who gives me strength."
~Philippians 4:13

With so much emphasis placed on winning, we might be a bit surprised when we are encouraged to lose something. Of course, we usually strive to be winners, but there are three areas of our lives in which losing is a good thing:

1. **The Past**—We all feel regret about certain things when we look back at our past. It's so easy to get caught up in the "what ifs" and the "if onlys." But Isaiah 43:18 tells us, *"forget the former things; do not dwell on the past."* What wonderful advice! By letting go of the past, we allow ourselves the freedom to appreciate today and look forward to tomorrow with anticipation. **Choose to lose** the past and its regrets. Make today a celebration of life!

2. **Anger**—It's so easy to become angry and bitter towards someone who has hurt us! Anger can turn our hearts away from God and keep us from true happiness. Anger, resentment, and bitterness are all toxic emotions, and the sad truth is, the longer we harbor those feelings, the more we hurt ourselves. Holding on to anger doesn't hurt the person it's directed toward; it only hurts us! Ephesians 4:31-32 says, *"Get rid of all bitterness, rage, and anger...along with every form of malice. Be kind and compassionate to one*

another, forgiving each other, just as in Christ God forgave you." We should tell ourselves every day to simply "let it go!" **Choose to lose** the devastation of anger!

3. Worry—We worry about a variety of things: family, friends, money, jobs, health, what might happen tomorrow, and the list goes on and on. If we really stop and think, can we say honestly that any of that worry has made one bit of difference in the situation that troubles us so much? Of course, it hasn't. Luke 12:25 says it beautifully: *"Who of you by worrying can add a single hour to his life?"* If we are "worry warts" and catch ourselves worrying so much about tomorrow that we take all the joy out of today, commit that verse to memory. **Choose to lose** the worry that robs us of the precious joy of today!

Challenge of the Day

Look at these three areas as they relate to your life and find one situation that you truly need to **lose** in order to make your life happier. How do you think you can accomplish that loss?

Day 54

Practice What You Preach

"How can you say to your brother, 'Let me take the speck out of your eye,' when all the time there is a plank in your own eye?" ~Matthew 7:4

Yvonne was a devoted Christian and often her friends came to her for advice. She was well known for having a good listening ear, giving solid Christian advice, and promising to be a prayer warrior. But this time, it was Yvonne who was struggling with life. Of course she knew God's promises, but all of a sudden, she found herself traveling a rugged road. As she curled up in bed with her Bible in one hand and a cup of hot chocolate in the other, she wondered what advice she would give a friend if they came to her with these difficult circumstances. Immediately, Mark 11:22 came to her mind, *"Have faith in God!"*

Many times it's so much easier to hand out advice when we see someone else in a bad situation. We can usually see things objectively and we want to help make it all better. However, when faced with our own difficulties, are we able to be so objective? Can we set aside our hurt feelings and try to see things from an advisor's perspective? Once Yvonne looked at her own situation, she realized that she had given this advice to many of her friends in similar circumstances. She knew then she needed to go to God and ask for His guidance. She didn't have to go through this ordeal alone, so she immediately went to God in prayer.

When we are traveling those rugged roads, do we go to God, search His word, or do we attempt to solve the situation on our own? Having faith and knowing that God is walking beside us is so important. In Hebrews 13:5, Paul reminds us of God's promise, that *"He will not leave us or forsake us."* What a comforting thought! We simply need faith. And like Yvonne, we must follow our own advice! We need to **practice what we preach!**

Challenge of the Day

Do you sincerely practice what you preach? When it is you who is struggling, do you give yourself the same advice that you often give others? Write about a time you gave advice to a friend when you needed to follow that advice yourself.

A Hot-Tempered Mess

"A hot-tempered person stirs up conflict, but the one who is patient calms a quarrel." ~Proverbs 15:18

Regina tried to smile to hide her embarrassment as her friend, Melinda, began to shout in anger. Unfortunately, this wasn't the first time Melinda had caused a scene in public as she lost her temper over something trivial. Today, the steak she ordered wasn't prepared to her satisfaction and she made a terrible fuss with the patient waiter, drawing unwanted attention from nearby patrons in the restaurant. When she got home after dinner, Regina thought long and hard about her relationship with Melinda. Because of her hot temper, Melinda was just no longer a pleasant companion. Regina asked herself, "Should I talk to her and ask her why she is such a **hot-tempered mess** or should I just forget about it and not be friends with her anymore?" After praying about it, she decided that as a Christian, she needed to try to help Melinda with a little "anger management," even if it meant possibly harming their friendship.

Regina chose an appropriate time and expressed her concern with her friend. She told her that "as a Christian, you need to be a positive role model to those around you. God doesn't want you to have all this pent-up anger, nor does He want you to display it publicly. Please try to think before you act."

When choosing our friends, it is wise to evaluate how they react to situations where patience and understanding are required. Do they "fly off the handle" **or** do they exercise restraint and handle the situation in a caring manner? There are many scriptures that deal with anger issues. Proverbs 29:22 tells us, *"a hot-tempered man stirs up dissension, but a patient man calms a quarrel."* And James makes it quite clear what kind of behavior God prefers when he writes, *"Everyone should be quick to listen, slow to speak and slow to become angry, for man's anger does not bring about the righteous life that God desires."* [James 1:19]

Having a "short fuse," acting and speaking out of anger without thinking, can cause many hurtful situations. If we know someone who has problems with anger management, share with them these helpful verses from God's Word. Pray for God's guidance, asking Him to help a friend avoid being a "hot-tempered mess!"

Challenge of the Day

Do you have a friend who exhibits a hot temper? As a Christian, do you feel an obligation to help that person or suggest a way for them to receive professional help? What are the consequences of having a hot-tempered friend?

Day 56

Getting Back Up

"If one falls down, his friend can help him up. But pity the man who falls and has no one to help him up!" ~Ecclesiastes 4:10

Ellen sat close to her friend, Jackie, and watched as huge tears rolled down her cheek. Ellen could hear the helplessness in Jackie's voice as she grieved the loss of her sister. But her sister was gone, another tragic victim of cancer, and Jackie was overcome with grief. They had always been incredibly close and now, through the flood of her tears, she was asking the million-dollar question, "How can I make it without my sister?"

Isn't it difficult to watch a friend who is experiencing grief? Many of us have faced similar situations in which we see a close friend grieving the loss of a loved one. It's difficult to find just the right words to bring comfort. We think, "Maybe I should just leave her alone. She'll get better eventually." But in terrible times like these, we need our Christian sisters to sit with us, listen to us, cry with us, encourage us. And just as importantly, we need to be there for a friend who is hurting to support her, comfort her, and show her compassion. Paul tells us in Galatians 6:2 that we should *"carry each other's burdens."* It may not be easy for us to deal with someone else's grief, but we should ask ourselves, "If I were grieving and heartbroken, wouldn't I want a 'sister' to help me get through that dark time? If I had fallen into the depths of despair, wouldn't I want someone who would sit with me, hold my hand as well as my heart, reach out and help me get back up on my feet?"

A true friend can give us hope again through the strength of her friendship and faith. She can bring our eyes up when we are looking down in grief, and remind us of how much God loves us. A real friend will always be there to reassure us of how much God cares and how much He wants to extend His powerful hand and help us **get back up!**

Challenge of the Day

Are you blessed with a friend who would help you get back up? And are YOU the kind of friend who would be there to help a friend when she needs you the most? When was the last time you helped a friend get back up?

"Through The Eyes Of Love"

"The Lord does not look at the things people look at.
People look at the outward appearance,
but the Lord looks at the heart.'"
~1 Samuel 16:7

How often do we look at others and base our judgment of them by their outward appearance? We've probably all heard the old saying, "You can't judge a book by its cover." How many times do we make snap judgments about people simply based on their appearance without taking the time to look beyond the façade, to try to see the real person underneath? We need to be looking at their hearts, not their haircuts!

Sometimes we admire someone who seems to have it so together. They wear nice clothes, always have their hair and makeup perfectly in place and give the impression that their lives are carefree. But if we could see into their hearts, we might see family issues, an abusive relationship, financial worries, a drinking problem, all hidden behind this mask of success. Then there is the flip side to this scenario. Someone who has a poor appearance, doesn't dress well, doesn't think or act like we think they should, doesn't travel in the same social circles, can turn out to be someone who has a true heart for God.

Jesus had something to say about being judgmental. He said, *"Do not judge, or you too will be judged. For in the same way you judge others, you will be judged, and with the measure you use, it will be measured to you."* [Matthew 7:1-2] And in John, He stated, *"Stop judging by mere appearances, and make a right judgment."* [John 7:24] Jesus wanted us to be willing to look past the pretense of fine attire that might hide a broken heart, or to see beyond the rough exterior that conceals a heart full of love. Either way, we need to try to see people through God's eyes, just as we want others to see **us**.

Are we willing to make the effort to see inside someone's heart instead of judging them by what is on the surface? We need to ask God to help us keep an open heart, to help us take the time to look into someone else's eyes and see their true heart just as God sees it. He wants us to always be **looking through the eyes of love.**

Challenge of the Day

Can you recall a time when you made the wrong judgment of a person based solely on their appearance? Think of someone you have misjudged and tell about how your opinion changed once you got to know them better.

Day 58

Green With Envy

*"Do not let your heart envy sinners, but always be zealous
for the fear of the Lord." ~Proverbs 23:17*

Young or old, male or female, most of us have been envious
of someone. Our society creates such a buzz around
Hollywood stars, professional athletes, politicians,
performing artists, and the rich and famous. If we are not
careful, we find ourselves coveting the lifestyles, body types and
material possessions of these "idols." Why is it that we
transform mere human beings into "gods" just because they
have gained some form of celebrity status? In many cases, these
idols may not be living lives that are acceptable in God's eyes.

Our envy may not necessarily be directed toward someone in the
spotlight. Perhaps we envy a co-worker who received a
promotion which she didn't truly deserve, or maybe it's a friend
who is always dressed in the trendiest fashions but is actually
living far beyond her means. While we know both of these
behaviors are not pleasing to God, a touch of envy might still
creep into our souls.

Envy can be a destructive emotion and coveting is a sin. Instead
of giving in to envy, we need to recognize it, rethink it, and then
regroup. We need to ask ourselves, "Is this situation something I

really want for myself, or is it just a temporary 'fix' to help me cope with some inner struggle? How would God perceive my dilemma?" Making the right decision, the one we know in our hearts to be one that would please God, will certainly give us more long-term happiness. In the meantime, we are being a shining example for Christ!

Challenge of the Day

In your circle of friends, is there anyone you envy? If so, why? What do you think God would say about this if He was discussing your situation with you over dinner?

Day 59

"Don't Worry, Be Happy!"

"Therefore do not worry about tomorrow,
for tomorrow will worry about itself." ~Matthew 6:34

Remember that funny reggae song from the 80's in which Bobby McFerrin kept reminding us not to worry, just to be happy? It was such a catchy tune with an easy Jamaican swing to it and the lyrics were so clever–it made you smile just to listen to it. But does it seem to you that in today's world we have so much more to worry about than our parents did back in their day? Of course, each generation had its own unique worries, but with technology changing our lives so quickly, it's hard to keep up. Sometimes we find ourselves wishing for the simple life of years past. Our parents didn't have a play-by-play of world affairs seconds after they occur nor did they have to worry about what their children had access to on the Internet. It just seems like everywhere we look today, there are problems that our parents and grandparents couldn't even have imagined.

Many people often find themselves worrying about all kinds of concerns that bombard our lives every day. But in Matthew 6:27, scripture tells us that worrying doesn't add a single hour to our life. The Bible clearly states that worrying is a futile exercise; it rarely changes the outcome of a situation. Worrying about tomorrow just takes away the joy that we could be experiencing today. Shouldn't we instead *"seek His kingdom and His righteousness"*? [Matthew 6:33]

Instead of focusing on worry that is basically unproductive, focus on God. He tells us, *"Do not worry about your life!"* [Matthew 6:25]   Our heavenly Father knows our needs. Like the song says, "Every night we have some trouble, but when you worry, you make it double!" We need to humble ourselves before God and ask him to place His hand upon us. Let go of that worry and be happy!

Challenge of the Day

Are you in a situation that causes you to worry? If so, write a prayer asking God to help you deal with it.

Lean On Him!

"Trust in the Lord with all your heart and lean not on your own understanding; in all your ways acknowledge him and he will make your paths straight." ~Proverbs 3:5-6

Isn't it amazing how trusting we were as little children? When our daddies threw us up in the air or swung us around in a circle, we had no fear because we knew he was going to catch us or make sure we were safe. There was never any doubt our daddy was going to be there no matter what. We trusted him with all our hearts.

Our heavenly Father expects us to trust Him just as we trusted our biological fathers when we were kids. But a sad thing often happens as we grow up—we lose that sense of complete trust because we encounter other relationships that disappoint and mislead us. We learn that not everyone is trustworthy and dependable. But isn't it a blessing to know God will never disappoint or give us any reason **not** to trust Him? He is always there, waiting to catch us whenever we fall.

As indicated in scripture, the Lord expects His children to trust Him with all of their hearts and to lean on Him, to have the same trusting relationship with Him that we had as a child. Unfortunately, how many times have we tried to make decisions or wander off in a new direction on our own? Sometimes we forget we can trust solely in God's wisdom and we fail to lean on Him for the directions we need. Wouldn't it be easier to totally trust and ask God to walk with us through our journeys?

There are times we feel we can't trust anyone, but God knows what is best for us. We must trust him completely. We should assume the blind trust of a child and go to our heavenly Father for His help. Then follow His lead and let Him guide us on our path. Learn to **lean on Him.** He will always be there to catch you!

Challenge of the Day

Can you remember an instance when you tried to do something on your own without consulting God's guidance? What happened as a result? Do you sometimes find it hard to be trusting, even with God?

Walking The Runway

"Remember your leaders, who spoke the word of God to you. Consider the outcome of their way of life and imitate their faith." ~Hebrews 13:7

Professional models are highly trained to make their walk down the runway memorable. Their distinctive style includes such things as perfect posture, the correct hip action, holding their head just right, keeping their arms close to their bodies, and constantly practicing "the walk." These models make a lasting impression, particularly on younger females who want to imitate them.

Even though most of us are not professional models, we do walk a runway of sorts each day. We may not always be aware of it, but we serve as models to those around us. Did you know that Timothy was led to Christ by his mother and grandmother? Yes, Timothy watched these two women walk the walk every day, and they made a lasting impression on him. They continually demonstrated what was important—their faith in God. They were the perfect role models for Timothy who later led a ministry that helped change the world. What might have happened to the development of Christianity if he had not had these amazing "models" in his life?

Do we ever wonder what our behavior says about us as we walk out on life's runway? In many cases, people are watching our walk to see if we will stumble. Others may see us as a blessing in their lives because we may be the only example of Christ-like behavior they ever see. Are we having a profound effect on those who are watching even when we are not aware of it? Do we see ourselves as strong role models of Christian values? We may not be famous runway models, but we can be super models for someone in our lives. We should be sure that when we walk down that runway of life, we are modeling the best of what Christ has to offer!

Challenge of the Day

Look around and see who is watching you as you walk the runway each day. Does it concern you that those people might be imitating your faith? What changes do you need to make to insure you are being a good role model for Christ?

Lavished With Love

"How great is the love the Father has lavished on us, that we should be called children of God! And that is what we are!" ~1 John 3:1

As Lydia sat on a park bench, she drew her knees up underneath her chin and wrapped her arms around her legs. She put her head down and just let her tears fall. Her stomach was in knots and her heart was ravaged with hurt and pain. "Why doesn't anyone love me?" she thought. "What have I done to deserve this?"

Unfortunately, most of us have felt that same empty, broken-hearted feeling at some point in our lives. When our pain feels like a sword through our hearts, we are filled with a multitude of emotions such as bitterness, profound loss, self-pity, devastating loneliness, or terrible failure. Those emotions can cause dramatic and debilitating consequences if we allow them to take over our hearts. Even though we may have suffered something this devastating, we need to try very hard to keep things in perspective. Easier said than done, right? How do we keep it in perspective when we are blinded by despair?

The answer, of course, is God. If we can turn our eyes away from our pain and turn them toward Him, we have His reassurance that we are never alone. We are His children, and

God, our Father, loves us in a way that is impossible for us to totally comprehend. As we are taught in scripture, God lavishes us with love. Even when we are distraught and disillusioned, we can rest assured that God's love for us is powerful and everlasting. His love is abounding and abundant. We are His children!

If we ever experience moments such as Lydia's, we simply must remember God is there for us! We need to allow Him to wrap His arms around us and lavish us with His love. There couldn't be a more comforting thought!

Challenge of the Day

Can you remember a time when your heart was filled with loneliness and despair? What steps did you take to overcome those feelings? Explain how God was involved in your recovery process.

Day 63

Friendship

"My command is this: Love each other as I have loved you. Greater love has no one than this, that he lay down his life for his friends."
~John 15: 12-13

In her book, *The Friendships of Women*, Dee Brestin talks about how important our women friends are to us. She illustrates the importance of these relationships as she cites examples from the Bible–Ruth and Naomi as well as Mary and Elizabeth. Even as little girls, she explains, we display a need to connect with other little girls—we hold hands, we hug, we share things heart to heart. And most of us carry that need to bond and be in close contact with other women into adulthood.

How different that is from the relationships that are formed between little boys. Boys play ball, wrestle, and keep their relationships at arm's length. And as adults, men tend to relate to each other as buddies–they use sports or business as a basis for friendship but often, this is all they have in common. They just don't frequently call up and say, "Hey, let's do lunch!" Isn't it amazing how very different we are! Another book that addresses this issue is, *"Men Are From Mars, Women Are From Venus."* Oh, how true that is!

No matter how close you are to your husband or sweetheart, there is nothing like the blessing we, as women, receive from the friendship of a close girlfriend. We all need that special BFF to be our confidante, our soul sister, the one who will support us, be our cheerleader, laugh with us, cry with us, celebrate our successes and help us pick up the pieces when our hearts are broken. There is just something miraculous about having a precious friend who is always there for us, no matter what the circumstances. Our **girlfriends** are surely one of God's ways of taking care of us!

Challenge of the Day

If you are blessed with a precious girlfriend who enriches your life, how can you let her know how very special she is to you? Share a time when she has been there for you either in celebration or in a difficult situation.

Day 64

Dress Rehearsal

"I am going there to prepare a place for you. And if I go and prepare a place for you, I will come back and take you to be with me that you also may be where I am." ~John 14:2-3

"**B**reak a leg!" Jeff, the director, said to the cast as he went to his director's chair to watch the dress rehearsal. After weeks of preparation, coaching the dialogue and helping the cast members with movement and blocking, he had done all that he could do. Now it was up to his cast to bring the show to life and perform it well. Tomorrow night was opening night and his heart was filled with a mixture of emotions. Working so closely with these people, he had formed a great relationship with his cast and crew; they seemed like family to him. He had really grown to love them in his own special way.

Our life on earth is similar to a dress rehearsal. Our director is none other than our heavenly Father. Just as in a play, the director guides the actors, gives them directions on how to act, when and where to move, how to speak. Isn't this what God has done for us? He's provided us with everything we need to live as Christians. Now it's up to us to get out there on life's stage and perform that dress rehearsal to the best of our ability. We are His cast and He loves us and desires nothing more than to be able to call us His children. Can you believe God loved us so much that He sent His only son to die on the cross for our sins?

How amazing it is to know that we are His children! He has blessed us beyond measure by giving us this magnificent dress rehearsal, preparing us for the big performance of eternal life. He has lavished us with love and wants nothing more than for our dress rehearsal on earth to be a "hit" because He wants to spend eternity with His beloved children. Whatever it takes to make our dress rehearsal a smash, let's do it! *"Bravo!"*

Challenge of the Day

Is your dress rehearsal going well on earth? When the curtains close, are you going to receive thunderous applause from God for a job well done? What can you do to insure your dress rehearsal is a huge "hit"?

Three Wishes

"But the father said to his servants, 'Quick, bring the best robe and put it on him. Put a ring on his finger...bring the fatted calf...let's feast and celebrate. For this son of mine was dead and is alive again; he was lost and is found!'" ~Luke 15:22-24

There once was a young man who was granted three wishes. Well, of course, they were the usual lineup—money, travel the world, do whatever he pleased. But these wishes weren't granted to him by a genie from a magic lamp. They were given to him by his father who happened to be a very wealthy man. His father gave the young man his entire inheritance and let him go. Of course, the young man squandered all the money, traveled around, partied, and did whatever he pleased. And with that lifestyle came lots of friends who wanted to join the fun. Sadly, the money finally ran out, the young man's friends deserted him, and he was left with nothing. The day he woke up lying with the pigs in the pigsty, he realized he had finally hit rock bottom and really needed to go back home and he did.

What kind of response did the young man receive when he got home? Did his father say, "Ha! I told you so!" or "Hey, you're not fit to be my son anymore."? No, his father embraced his son and was so happy to see him that he threw a big party to celebrate his homecoming.

Why do you think Jesus told this story? He wanted us to compare the father in the story to God and **us** to that son who made so many bad choices. Yes, we often make bad choices just like that young man, but the wonderful thing is, our heavenly Father is always willing to forgive us and welcome us back with open arms! All we have to do is ask for His forgiveness and God is completely willing to accept our repentant heart. Isn't that wonderful? Of course, we're bound to make bad choices because we're human; but how blessed we are that we have a loving Father who will always take us back when we come home!

Challenge of the Day

Has there been a time in your life when you have wandered away from God because of some bad choices? What were your bad choices? Were you able to ask for God's forgiveness? If so, do you feel that you have been truly forgiven?

Day 66

Layers Of Life

"Therefore, prepare your minds for action; be self-controlled; set your hope fully on the grace to be given you when Jesus Christ is revealed. As obedient children, do not conform to the evil desires you had when you lived in ignorance...be holy in all you do." ~1 Peter 1:13-15

When living in a cold climate, we have learned that it's best to "layer up" in the winter. That simply means we put on several layers of clothing. If perhaps we enter a warm room or the sun pops out unexpectedly, we can shed a few layers to be more comfortable. Our goal is comfort during those unpredictable winter days, not necessarily the most fashionable time of year!

Similarly, life can cause us to add "layers" as well. As we mature, we add layers of emotions due to the experiences we encounter along the way. These can be layers of turmoil, confusion, or tragedy. Bad experiences can often leave us with many layers of negativity—excess baggage that weighs us down and makes life difficult. The good news is God can help us shed those layers of guilt or strife, something similar to a refining process. We just have to be willing to trust in Him, communicate with Him, and let Him direct our life's journeys. When we step into the warmth of His love, we can shed those unnecessary layers that keep us from being the person God wants us to be.

When we rid ourselves of the negative "layers" that build up throughout our lives, a miraculous transformation can occur:

- We learn to trust and develop more **faith** in God.
- We become more determined and develop our abilities to **persevere.**
- We exhibit the **courage** to stand firm in our beliefs.

Our goal in life should be to shed any negative or evil layers the world inflicts upon us. We should always strive to bask in the warmth of the Holy Spirit, so much so that those excess layers become unimportant. Once we shed those layers, we get down to the foundation of our faith which is the most important "layer" of all—God!

Challenge of the Day

When you look at yourself honestly, do you see layers of negativity you would like to shed? What are they and what can you do to remove those layers from your life?

God's Punctuation: Period Or Comma?

"Be joyful always; pray continually; give thanks in all circumstances for this is God's will for you in Jesus Christ." ~1 Thessalonians 5:16-17

Kendra was so hopeful that her new relationship with Cory would work. However, there just seemed to be too many issues on which they disagreed and too many doubts began flooding her mind. She asked God to help with her situation as she prayed, "I have way too much love to live my life alone! What should I do, Lord?" After several months, she realized God had replaced the question mark at the end of her prayer with a period. The relationship was over.

Much like Kendra, we all experience doubts and questions in life. Sometimes we think God has put a period at the end of our prayer and that our dreams are over and done. But when God doesn't answer our prayers as quickly as we think He should or in the way we hope, perhaps God has merely changed the punctuation from a period to a comma which means, "Just wait a second, be patient, He's not quite finished with the answer to that prayer."

Just because God doesn't answer us immediately or things don't work out as **we** had planned doesn't mean God does not know our hearts. Do we ever consider that God is possibly saving us from a major disaster or possibly **He** has something bigger and better in store for us? Why don't we try looking at our disappointment in a more positive light? Remember, **God knows best**!

When disappointment or confusion comes our way, we need to get rid of that period which takes away our hope. Instead, try using a comma because God is not finished with us yet. He is already looking ahead to the next page of our lives. Let Him take away those periods and question marks in our hearts and replace them with exclamations of joy! Watch for God's perfect punctuation!

Challenge of the Day

Have you been disappointed God didn't answer a prayer as you wanted? What action did you take? Do you believe you can be patient and let God take care of you in His own time?

The "Only Child"

"And he has given us this command: Whoever loves God
must also love his brother." ~1 John 4:21

Many of us are fortunate enough to have siblings. There is
no other relationship like the bond between brothers and
sisters. With them, we share cherished memories that
cannot be understood by anyone else. We share the same
parental heritage, the same "gene pool," and hopefully, as we
have aged, that family tie has only grown stronger.

But what about being an "only child"? Certainly there are some
advantages to being the little darling of the family, the one upon
whom parents and grandparents lavish their attention and
affection. Unfortunately, being an only child also comes with
some disadvantages simply because that child is deprived of the
special relationship shared with a sibling.

There is another relationship that, as women, we are equally
blessed to experience in life and that is the special bond we have
with our sisters in Christ. Let's take a moment and think about
the women God has placed in our lives, the special ones who
have shared our life journeys. Hopefully, there has been a
sister/friend who has been there for us through the best of times
as well as the worst of times…a girlfriend who has become a
"soul sister."

"Time passes. Life happens. Distance separates. Children grow up. Jobs come and go. Love waxes and wanes. Hearts break. Parents die. Colleagues forget favors. Careers end. Men don't always do what they are supposed to do. But our sisters are there, no matter how much time and how many miles are between you. A girlfriend is never farther away than needing her can reach...The women in our lives are there, cheering us on, praying for us, pulling for us, and waiting with open arms when we need them the most." ~(Author Unknown)

How blessed we are to have these wonderful women in our lives, our "adopted" sisters. Our lives just wouldn't be the same without them. As sisters in Christ, we experience the blessings of God's love because we are His children. It is truly a gift from God NOT to be an "only child!"

Challenge of the Day

As you look back, do you recognize how God has placed special women in your life to walk with you through the hills and valleys? Have you had the opportunity to be this kind of "soul sister" to someone else? Describe that relationship.

Bitterness

"Get rid of all bitterness, rage and anger, brawling and slander, along with every form of malice. Be kind and compassionate to one another, forgiving each other, just as in Christ, God forgave you." ~Ephesians 4:31-32

Emma and Sherry had been friends since kindergarten. They lived just a few blocks from each other and remained friends all the way through high school. Though Sherry went away to college and Emma stayed home, they kept in close contact. Emma even asked Sherry to be the maid of honor at her wedding. But because of a terrible misunderstanding, the friends exchanged angry words and the friendship ended in bitterness and broken hearts. The two girls never spoke to each other again.

When someone we care about hurts us, we often tend to be angry, resentful, and bitter toward that person. Isn't it sad that these unfortunate situations occur? However, the real truth is we have all experienced these emotions at some time in our lives, the feelings that Paul described as **bitterness, rage, and anger.**

Remember those bracelets that were popular several years ago, WWJD (What Would Jesus Do)? In a situation like this, what **would** Jesus do? Would He be critical, angry or bitter and lash out at His friends? Would He shout malicious, hurtful words that could never be taken back? Did He ever gossip or seek revenge? No, Jesus was in all instances loving, forgiving, compassionate, and understanding even when someone broke His heart.

A lost friendship, even a broken marriage, can cause us to have such terrible feelings of betrayal, anger, and bitterness. Trying to forgive someone who has caused those painful feelings can be incredibly difficult. Many of us still carry the scars of a hurting heart and find it impossible to let them heal. Can we forgive someone who has hurt us and rid ourselves of the anger and bitterness that we feel toward them? If not, we need to ask God to help us do that. We should let God show us the way to free ourselves of these toxic emotions. With His help, we can do it!

Challenge of the Day

Are you holding bitterness or anger in your heart against someone? How can you make those negative feelings go away?

Day 70

Run, Susan, Run!

"Ask and it will be given to you; seek and you will find; knock and the door will be opened to you." ~Matthew 7:7

The divorce had been a long, heart-wrenching experience for Susan. Her world had been turned upside down and she just couldn't see much of a future for herself. She decided the best thing for her to do was to move to a different city. After all, her ex-husband's family was deeply rooted in the town where they had lived, so she felt like she needed a new beginning, a fresh start. While it seemed to be the perfect solution, Susan had such mixed emotions about it all. Moving would never take away the hurt. Even worse, it would move her away from all of her friends, colleagues, and church. These people were going to be her support system which she would desperately need in the days ahead.

When we find our world has totally fallen apart for any number of reasons, can we really run away from it? No, of course, we can't. When we get unpacked, the problems are right there in the suitcase with us. What should we do? Where can we turn? Who is there to pick us up and help us move forward? The answer is God.

In Matthew, Jesus tells us all we have to do is knock and the door will be opened for us. In other words, all we have to do is look to God for help when we are in trouble, and He is on the other side of the door, waiting with open arms. Jesus is telling us that faith and trust in God are the keys to dealing with tough situations. Believing in God's power will give us strength, courage, forgiveness, healing, comfort, and love. What more could we ask?

Remember the old cliché "you can run but you can't hide"? Trying to run away from our problems doesn't make them any easier to face. But knocking on God's door is the first step towards healing. We need to allow Him to enfold us in His love and let Him help us get through any terrible struggles we may encounter. There's no reason to run away from God!

Challenge of the Day

Have you ever felt the need to just run away from your problems? What did you do? What advice would you give someone like Susan?

Inheritance

*"Into an inheritance that can never perish, spoil, or fade—
kept in heaven for you."* ~1 Peter 1:4

Dottie picked up a magazine while she waited patiently in the doctor's office. As she thumbed through the articles, she stopped and read one about a very rich man who shared his amazing story. "I got off at the train depot one day as a tramp. For a year I had begged on the streets. Badly in need of food, I touched a man on the shoulder and said, 'Mister, please give me a dime.' As soon as I saw his face, I recognized my aging father. 'Don't you know me?' I asked. Throwing his arms around me, he cried, 'Oh, my son, I have found you at last! All I have is yours!' Think of it—I was a tramp who begged for 10 cents from a man I didn't know was my father, when for 18 years he had been looking for me to give me all he possessed!"

If someone told us that we were included in a relative's will and we would be inheriting millions of dollars, what would our reactions be? After we picked ourselves up off the floor, most of us would be speechless and thrilled beyond measure. However, as Christians, we have something far more valuable. We have the wealth of God that has been promised to us, and it is an inheritance that can never perish! It is incorruptible and eternal.

Isn't there something miraculous in knowing that our Father has given us an inheritance of eternal life in the kingdom of heaven? Paul also mentions this precious gift in Colossians 1:12 when he writes, "*giving thanks to the Father who has qualified you to share in the inheritance of the saints in the kingdom of light.*" Now **that is an inheritance!**

Some of us may have friends who are not aware, who do not fully realize what they have "in Christ." If so, please share with them about their vast spiritual wealth and inheritance they are promised by their Father. And as for us, if we are true believers and followers of Christ, we can rest assured that an inheritance beyond our most incredible dreams awaits us—that's a promise!

Challenge of the Day

Have you ever unexpectedly inherited something precious or valuable from a relative? If so, what was it? Compare an inheritance of earthly "things" to the inheritance that you are promised from God. What is the difference?

Day 72

The Grass Is Greener

*"A heart at peace gives life to the body,
but envy rots the bones." ~Proverbs 14:30*

As Caroline climbed into her car after work, she felt a twinge of jealousy. Her single friends were going out for the evening, and she wanted so much to be going with them. But she needed to go home and prepare dinner for her husband. Of course, she loved her husband very much, but deep down in her heart, she did sometimes miss the carefree days of single life.

Oh, doesn't "the grass always looks greener on the other side of the fence"? But, guess what? Often, there are just as many brown spots over there too! Unfortunately, there are times when we are not totally happy with every aspect of our lives. Regardless of which side of the fence we are on, there are just certain things that appear to be better for other people when we view them from afar. We have a tendency to want what we do not or cannot have.

Jealousy is such a common emotion, no matter who we are. Married people want to be single; single people want to be married. People who live in cold climates want to live where it's warm; people who live in warm climates want to go where it's

146

cool. The examples are endless. Fortunately, those of us who know Christ realize that when our hearts feel a hint of jealousy, all we have to do is look to Christ for guidance. Instead of always wanting something we don't have, wouldn't we be happier people if we focused that energy toward all the precious gifts we **do** possess?

Always keep in mind our Creator made each of us in our own unique way. We are all important to Him and we should be focusing on utilizing our God-given talents to complete the task He set before us. Instead of worrying about success, fame, or popularity, or being envious and wishing we were someone or someplace else, just take a look around at all the green He has put on **our** side of the fence!

Challenge of the Day

Can you describe a time in your life when you thought the grass was greener on someone else's side of the fence? What were the circumstances? What did you do when you felt that twinge of jealousy? What were the results of your actions?

Make It A Great Day!

"This is the day the Lord has made; let us rejoice and be glad in it." ~Psalm 118:24

Nancy smiled as she quieted her noisy classroom so they could hear the morning announcements. It was the beginning of a typical school day, and the students listened to the booming voice of the principal as he listed all the upcoming events for the week. But every day he concluded his announcements with this challenge to the students, "Make it a great day or not, the choice is yours!" He set the tone for everyone to have a great day at school.

What do we do to set the tone for our day? Do we make a conscious choice of whether or not we're going to make it a great day? Do we take a little quiet time each morning to read a short devotion with that first cup of coffee? Or maybe we sit outside and just watch nature for a few minutes while we eat breakfast. Taking the time to enjoy, reflect, and contemplate the happenings in our lives can bring us peace and a greater understanding of our life's direction.

Unfortunately, many of us begin the day by meeting the demands of the clock: running out the door, grabbing a cup of coffee or juice to go, barely getting the kids off to school, or rushing into the office just in time for a big meeting or to make a pressing deadline. Our lives today are extremely hectic and complex. When do we ever take quiet time for ourselves, the time we need to keep life in perspective? We need some time to renew our faith, refresh our hearts—a little time for God.

Is it possible for us to spend some quiet time each morning with God? Perhaps we are not "morning people" but the results would be well worth the effort. Why not try getting up a few minutes early, getting a good devotional book, pouring a flavored coffee or a delicious hot cup of tea, and turning our hearts in God's direction. We can set the tone for our day and make it wonderful. **"Make it a great day or not, the choice is ours!"**

Challenge of the Day

When you look at your busy schedule, do you see a time you could set aside to visit with God each day? Decide what adjustments you need to make in order for that to happen.

Day 74

Father Knows Best

"Charm is deceptive, and beauty is fleeting; but a woman who fears the Lord is to be praised." ~Proverbs 31:30

During the 50's and 60's, the early days of television, it's interesting to see how popular TV shows portrayed women. Characters like Jane Wyatt on "Father Knows Best" or June Cleaver, Donna Reed, and Harriet Nelson were supposed to be typical American housewives. Their houses were always immaculate; they could handle any crisis with ease. They were all a size 6 and their hair and makeup were always perfect. They kept busy around the house wearing high heels, a perfectly ironed shirtwaist dress and never broke a sweat! Their husbands came home every night to a hot, delicious dinner, perfectly prepared and served to the happy family. There was always laughing and talking as they were seated around the dinner table. Ah, those were the days! Or were they?

Those stereotypical images of the perfect wife and mother were truly figments of someone's vivid imagination. Perhaps those women existed back then, but it's unlikely that June Cleaver is still around today. Times have changed so much and today's woman has assumed a very different role in the world. She has truly "come a long way, Baby." Many times she is not only a wife and mother but perhaps a student, a career woman, a political leader, a business woman, doctor, educator, lawyer, or scientist. The opportunities open for women now were unheard of in Ozzie and Harriet's day.

And what does the woman of today need now more than ever? She needs to remember that no matter what role she assumes in life, her focus needs to stay on her heavenly Father. With women's lives being pulled in so many directions and with so many more responsibilities, life can become so hectic we sometimes lose our grip on our faith. Sometimes, there just isn't enough time. That's why, as today's Christian women, we must keep ourselves grounded in the Word. Can we take some time out of our busy days to pray, to think about our blessings, to close our eyes, be still and know that He is God? The Lord loves us no matter what role in life we have chosen. We may not be the perfect woman, but please remember—our heavenly **Father Knows Best!**

Challenge of the Day

During your busy day, do you find it hard to set aside time to be with God? How could you adjust your schedule so that you can develop a closer walk with your heavenly Father?

Day 75

Decisions, Decisions, Decisions!

*"Have I not commanded you? Be strong and courageous. Do not be
frightened; do not be discouraged, for the Lord your God will be with you
wherever you go." ~Joshua 1:9*

A message that appeared on Lori's Facebook page said, "The decisions you make today shape your life tomorrow." What a reminder for Lori as she was facing some difficult decisions in her own life. For several months, Lori knew in her heart that she was addicted to pain medication. It was such an innocent process; initially, the medication was prescribed after her surgery. Now, only a few months later, she thought she couldn't live without it. Her addiction was beginning to affect her work and her relationship with her family. She realized she had to seek help or face losing everything she loved.

Unfortunately, this scenario is all too common in our world today. Doctors prescribe pain medication to help their patients deal with the extreme pain of post-surgery, but often patients misuse the drugs and become reliant on them. Then the decision arises—do they have the courage to go and seek the help they need to become "normal" again, or do they continue on the downward spiral caused by the addiction? When faced with this decision, it may take an intervention from a friend or family member, but it can't be an easy one to face alone.

A person who is battling an addiction of any kind, whether it's drugs, alcohol, food, or gambling, needs help to break the terrible, self-destructive cycle. God knows when we are at a weak point in our lives, and He wants to help us become the person He intends us to be. This is not possible if we are relying on some substance or activity that doesn't include Him. He wants us to gain the strength it takes to fight our addictions by seeking help from those who are ready and willing to guide us to His power. No one needs to face these challenges alone. God is there for us. He's just waiting for us to make that important decision to reach out to Him for courage and His loving support. The decision to look up to Him is up to us!

Challenge of the Day

Have you ever been addicted to something? If so, how did you overcome your addiction? If you were counseling a friend who was suffering from an addiction, what would your advice be as a Christian friend?

Day 76

This Little Light Of Mine

"You are the light of the world. A city built on a hill cannot be hidden. Neither do people light a lamp and put it under a bowl. Instead they put it on its stand, and it gives light to everyone in the house. In the same way, let your light shine before men, that they may see your good deeds and praise your Father in heaven." ~Matthew 5:14-16

His team was playing for the division championship. The TV camera zoomed in for a close-up of his face. This well-known football player wept as someone sang the national anthem. When it was over, his teary eyes went toward heaven and he mouthed the words, "Thank you, my Father." After winning the game, he commented to the reporters, "God doesn't make mistakes. He's never made one mistake; God is so amazing." Quite a testament coming from a professional football player!

At a young age, this same player had been in serious trouble with law enforcement, but 15 years later, his coach commented, "He's a different man than he was when he was 22. It's a great thing for kids to see. It's a great thing for fathers to see. It's a very special deal."

Obviously, this "new-born" player has a heart for God. With all the notoriety that comes with professional sports, he has chosen

154

to *"let his light shine before men,"* just as the scripture describes. However, not all of us have the luxury of having our name up in lights to create a shining example for others. Praise God there are those who do use their "fortune and fame" to serve God. How often do we see a professional athlete point to heaven and thank God when he or she makes a great play? How many players share their wealth with those less fortunate in their communities? Those are the kinds of athletes that are letting their lights shine for the glory of God!

Does that mean we don't have to concern ourselves with our little lights? Absolutely not! Each of us can touch people's lives in a way this high-caliber player will never have the opportunity to reach. Through our actions, words, and service to others, we are a direct reflection of God. People need to see our love for God shining through us like a brilliant light. Are we using our little lamps to help change someone else's darkness? Let's ask God to use us for His glory! Then, as the coach said, "It'll be a special deal!"

Challenge of the Day

Are you a shining example of God's love? How do you show it? Who are you influencing today with your light?

A "Just Fine" Attitude

*"God will bring every act to judgment, everything which is hidden,
whether it is good or evil." ~Ecclesiastes 12:14*

As a mother, Mary Lynn's heart hurt for her daughter. Cynthia had been raised in a Christian home, but now that she was grown and living her own life, she had definitely veered away from her solid upbringing. Each time Mary Lynn tried to discuss her spiritual life with her, Cynthia would try to avoid the conversation. Mary Lynn wanted so badly to talk to Cynthia about her recent poor choices, her circumstances, and the turmoil and consequences which had resulted from these actions, but Cynthia's usual response was, "Oh, I am just fine, Mom!" In other words, "Leave me alone, mind your own business!"

It's so difficult to watch someone we love traveling down the wrong path, but often there is little we can do to change their direction. It's simply something they need to discover for themselves. The best we can do is pray they will soon find the right direction. Scripture clearly teaches us that God will bring every act to judgment. We must remember our Maker has the right to hold us accountable for **everything** we do, whether it's good or bad. Whatever path we choose, God knows our circumstances, decisions, and actions. We can't just ignore what Jesus taught us about living an obedient life. If we truly are children of God, we should be concerned with having the right attitude and making sound decisions based on His teachings.

Ultimately, when we stand before God, how do you think he will handle the *"everything is fine"* attitude? When we realize that God knows our hearts, our every thought and deed, we can only imagine what it will be like when He confronts us about our attitude. If we have an *"I am just fine attitude,"* then maybe it is time for an attitude adjustment.

Let's praise God for teaching us the true meaning of *"just fine."*

Challenge of the Day

Have you ever had an *"Oh, everything is just fine!"* attitude? Is everything really fine, or are you just trying to hide the truth? If God held you accountable today, would He be pleased with your attitude?

Day 78

Divine Obsession

"Why, you do not even know what will happen tomorrow. What is your life? You are a mist that appears for a little while and then vanishes."
~James 4:14

In modern psychology, the phrase "obsessive compulsive" has become a well-known term. Many people often become fixated on certain objects or events. While some people are obsessed with cars, hobbies, shopping, or sports, others are consumed with watching the weather report, their favorite TV shows, or their children's activities. When we become obsessed with specific areas of our lives, we tend to lose focus on what should be our most important obsession, God.

We all know our relationship with God should be our top priority and we are to love Him and serve accordingly. However, in the hurry-up world we live in today, sometimes God gets lost in the "busyness" of our lives. We find ourselves thinking, "I'll read my Bible some other time when it's quiet. I've just got too much else to do right now!" Or, "Let's just wait until next week to go to church. I don't want to miss the football game today!" When we let our obsession with everyday activities consume our thoughts, we often push God aside and that weakens our relationship with Him. He is no longer our top priority as He was when we first accepted Him as our Savior.

James reminds us that our lives are simply a mist—we are here today and gone tomorrow. We don't know what the future holds. Tomorrow we could receive a life-threatening health diagnosis or have a tragic accident that would change our lives forever. Would it take something as drastic as this to bring our priorities back to God? Let's think about what we may have become fixated on, what we may be obsessed with on a daily basis. Is it some object or activity that only brings temporary enjoyment? Or do we have an obsession that is fixated on our relationship with God? A **divine obsession** brings joy that is everlasting and eternal!

Challenge of the Day

Are you fixated on Jesus? If not, what have you allowed to become your obsession? What changes can you make in your life so that you are more focused on your heavenly Father?

Freedom To Choose

"Be careful, however, that the exercise of your freedom does not become a stumbling block to the weak." ~1 Corinthians 8:9

Looking back over the past week, Lisa kept asking herself, "How could I have done something so stupid? I knew better! I just made a bad choice! And what kind of example have I set for my friends?" She knew it was not a decision that would please God. Lisa had made a choice that resulted in hurt feelings and damaged relationships.

We all know God has given us the freedom to make choices. And whether those choices are good or bad is a direct reflection of who we are as Christians. Often we don't realize that our choices can have a profound impact on those around us as well—our families, our friends, our colleagues. When we make a decision or a choice that hasn't been carefully and prayerfully considered, it can have a ripple effect that brings our faith into question.

Whether or not we choose to believe it, other people are watching us. We need to stop and consider what kind of example we are setting for those around us. According to scripture, we need to be careful that our freedom or the choices we make do not cause others to stumble. Remember that our Christian influence can be seen in the words that are spoken from our lips, in our actions and reactions in certain situations, and the manner in which we deal with and respond to the difficult times in our lives. We certainly do not want to cause a friend or family member to "stumble" because we have not followed God's teachings. We want others to see in us the grace and wisdom that comes with putting God first in whatever choices we make. We can't let our bad choices have a negative influence on someone else's faith.

Be thankful God granted us the freedom to choose our own pathways in life, but also be mindful that our choices should be guided by His word and the example of Christ. Rather than being a stumbling block in someone else's pathway to God, let's try to be a positive Christian influence on those who see us every day.

Challenge of the Day

Can you remember a time when you were not a positive Christian role model for those around you? When you have a difficult choice to make, do you ask for God's help in making that decision?

I'm Just Me!

"Live as children of light (for the fruit of the light consists in all goodness, righteousness and truth) and find out what pleases the Lord."
~Ephesians 5:8-10

Two colleagues were working a display booth at a corporate conference. Because they worked in different departments, the two ladies were simply acquaintances, not close friends. However, after two days of talking nonstop to conference participants as well as each other, they became much better acquainted. As they were packing up the display, Kimberly remarked, "Carol, you have such a sweet, kind spirit." And Carol replied, "Oh Kimberly, you're so kind. I really don't try to be anything I am not. I'm just me. It has been such a joy to get to know you better."

Later back in the office, Kimberly kept hearing Carol's words, "I really don't try to be anything I am not. I'm just me." Kimberly wondered, "What is it that Carol has that I don't? What is it that draws people to her and makes her so naturally compelling? I wish I had a loving heart like Carol's!"

What is it that Carol has? What is it that makes her uniquely attractive to others? Obviously, she has a burning heart for God. Carol is blessed with a spirit that allows her to shine for her heavenly Father.

Do we ever find ourselves in this position? When we compare ourselves to our friends or acquaintances, do we feel a bit nervous or inferior? Do we feel as though we come up short spiritually? Do people see in us a heart and soul that shine for God? Do we draw others to us because they see God in us?

If not, we are encouraged to present ourselves in a way that is pleasing to God as well as to the people we come in contact with every day. And we can say to ourselves, "Oh, I'm just me," knowing that "**me**" is a shining example for Jesus Christ!

Challenge of the Day

"I am just me." Are you happy with the "me" you are today? Why, or why not? What can you do to make "me" a better example to others for Christ?

God Is The One And Only

"Do not worship any other god, for the Lord, whose name is Jealous, is a jealous God." ~Exodus 34:14

God is jealous? Wait a minute, how could that be true? We have been taught that jealousy is a sin. How can this scripture say that God is jealous? In the book of Exodus, God is giving His law to the Israelites and teaching them not to worship false gods, whether they are some sort of idol, material possessions, or even other people. He wanted to make it clear they must be completely devoted to Him. As He gave Moses the Ten Commandments, God said, *"You shall have no other gods before me."* [Exodus 20:3]

We must realize the term "jealous" as it is used in this context has a slightly different meaning than the one we commonly use. Webster's Dictionary defines this type of jealousy as "demanding exclusive loyalty." God isn't jealous like humans are jealous. He is not envious or covetous as we can be at times. Think of it this way: as a parent of a child who is the love of our life, how would we feel if he/she decided we were not a good enough parent? We would watch in disbelief as this child turned against us and chose to share his/her love and life with another adult, another "parent" figure. Most likely, we would be heartbroken.

In the same way, God is probably heartbroken when He watches His children worship another god, something that we have found to replace Him. What becomes our false god is anything we put before the **one and only** *God.* It might be money, power, possessions, or even other people. Whatever we give highest importance to in our lives becomes our false god; that's why God is a jealous God. He demands our love, our service, and our loyalty to Him alone. **He is the one and only God!**

In Matthew 4:10, Jesus said, *"Worship the Lord your God, and serve him only."* Are we serving God today? When he looks at us, His children, is He delighted to see a faithful servant? Is He our One and Only?

Challenge of the Day

Is there anything or anyone in your life who you place more emphasis on than God? If so, what is it and why is it so important to you?

Day 82

A "Doubting Thomas"

"Jesus replied, 'Truly I tell you, if you have faith and do not doubt, not only can you do what was done to the fig tree, but also you can say to this mountain, 'Go, throw yourself into the sea,' and it will be done."
~Matthew 21:21

Once Joanie accepted Christ as her savior, she felt an abundance of peace and thought that now she would see fewer problems in her life. However, as she struggled to balance her checkbook, she once again found herself a few hundred dollars short of meeting her monthly bills. She had reached a stage of Godly doubt. Joanie simply couldn't understand why, now that she had become a Christian, God wasn't smoothing out her life the way she expected. "Why would God, who is supposed to love me, put me through such financial hardships month after month?" she wondered. She found herself doubting God's love for her and became angry with Him.

We often wonder if God is really listening. Does He hear us? Does He feel our hurt? Does He know we need His help? The answer is yes, of course He does. Our God is an all-knowing, loving God. But does that mean He is going to make our lives easy or give us everything we want? The answer to this question is no, of course not. We are taught that God loves us as His children. But having faith in God does not mean we get a free ride for life. He has given us free will and that means that we are able to choose our own paths in life. When we make bad choices, we pay a price but we can still be assured of God's love for us. He's still there, even when we suffer through trials and tribulations. Those are often a means for us to learn, grow, and mature in our faith. We simply have to trust that God is always there for us; there should never be any doubt of that!

Remember Thomas, the disciple who just couldn't believe that Jesus had risen from the grave? He insisted that he was not going to believe it until he saw it for himself. When Jesus did appear to Thomas, He said, *"Because you have seen me, you have believed; blessed are those who have **not** seen and yet have believed."* [John 20:29] We must not let ourselves become a "Doubting Thomas." No matter our circumstances, there should be **no doubt** that God loves us and will be there for us...we just have to believe!

Challenge of the Day

Have you ever doubted God when you have experienced tough times? Were you able to overcome your doubt? What advice would you give someone who is suffering through trials and tribulations?

167

Heart Of A Servant

"Each one should use whatever gift he has received to serve others, faithfully administering God's grace in its various forms...If anyone serves, he should do it with the strength God provides, so that in all things God may be praised through Jesus Christ." ~1 Peter 4:10-11

Serving God with a humble spirit is an honor and a privilege. God has blessed each of us with different talents, strengths, and abilities. In this passage, Peter explains that we are to utilize our gifts to serve others and to bring glory to God.

Let's stop and think...what talents and skills have we been blessed with in our lives? The wonderful news is that God made each of us with our own unique gifts and talents. We are all different and have the ability to serve God in many ways. Even Paul speaks of this in Romans 12:6-8. *"We have different gifts according to the grace given us. If a man's gift is prophesying, let him use it in proportion to his faith. If it is serving, let him serve; if it is teaching, let him teach; if it is encouraging, let him encourage; if it is contributing to the needs of others, let him give generously; if it is leadership, let him govern diligently; if it is showing mercy, let him do it cheerfully."*

Wherever our talents lie, we are all called to serve, remembering to give God the glory. In other words, we should serve with **a servant's heart**. Even Jesus said He came to serve, not to be served. And when we use our talents, we must make sure the attention is not on us. We are merely the catalyst who is serving others for one reason—to bring glory to God.

Each of us has a part to play in furthering God's kingdom. We all have a vital role in the completion of God's work. Let's praise God today for giving us the gifts and talents to serve Him with our whole hearts!

Challenge of the Day

Make a list of the talents and abilities you are utilizing to serve and glorify God. Describe how you are using your God-given gifts.

Timing Is Everything

"Because he is at my right hand, I will not be shaken." ~Psalm 16:8

Each time Colleen went for chemotherapy, she took along her Bible and a journal. During one treatment, Colleen was composing a prayer list in her journal while the chemo "cocktail" was running through her veins. One of her favorite nurses, Christy, came to check her IV and before she knew it, Christy was asking for prayer. Christy, who had been married for several years to an extremely career-oriented man, was struggling with her marriage. As Christy began to share, tears welled up in Colleen's eyes—not because of the toxic chemicals that were being spread throughout her body, but because of the toxic story she was listening to as Christy shared her deteriorating marital situation. Needless to say, Colleen mentored her, read scripture and prayed with her. And of course, she added her name to the prayer list in her journal.

Isn't it interesting how God uses us to witness to others at some of the most inopportune times? Timing is everything! In the midst of the emotional and physical rollercoaster in Colleen's life, He used her to be a solid rock for Christy. As she shared with Christy, it was also a strong reminder to Colleen that God was at **her** right hand too, and she should not be shaken just as it says in scripture.

It is sometimes easy to become so consumed with our own issues, we tend to forget that others may be going through struggles of their own. Everyone has a story and God loves for us to share His strength and encouragement with those who need to hear it. He calls upon us as Christians to show His love, no matter the time or place. Just like Colleen who, in the middle of her own struggle, took time out to serve God and reach out to another hurting soul like Christy. **Any time is the right time** to show God's love!

Challenge of the Day

Can you remember a time when you were in turmoil, but you took time to witness or serve someone else's needs? Who could you add to your prayer journal right now? Why?

Friends Who "Stick"

"A man of many companions may come to ruin, but there is a friend who sticks closer than a brother." ~Proverbs 18:24

In the past few months, Sandy seemed to be developing a close relationship with Cheryl. When they got together, they chatted about family, children, their childhoods, health, exercise, and even church. Sandy was sure her friendship with Cheryl would be a long-lasting one because it seemed they had so much in common. Both women appeared to have their priorities in order: God, family, friends.

However, today Sandy's heart is broken. After some difficulties in Sandy's life, Cheryl turned her back on her friend and became a stranger. "Why does this always happen to me? Am I naive? Why do I always think the best of people and then get so disappointed? Is there something wrong with me?" thought Sandy.

Relationships make the world go around! Unfortunately, we've all had those "friends" who talk a good game, but when the chips are down, they're out the door! Then it's up to us to decide if we wish to continue that friendship or move on. Sometimes being betrayed by a "friend" can be devastating and we wonder if it's something we have done. Praying about this situation can truly help. Ask God for His help in dealing with your relationships. We should ask God to put someone in our lives who will be a true friend, one who will "stick!"

We all need friends. God made us the sociable creatures we are so that we would seek out the companionship of others. And if we have been blessed with one or two really close friends, we have been doubly blessed. We all need that soul mate who will laugh with us, cry with us, pray for us, and love us unconditionally, a friend who will "stick" with us through thick and thin. And just as importantly, pray that God will help **us** to be a friend who "sticks!"

Challenge of the Day

Have you ever felt betrayed by a friend? Has there ever been a time when **you** have betrayed a friend? What were the circumstances in both situations? Which one of your friends will "stick" with you through the good times and the bad?

Crossing The Finish Line

"I have fought the good fight, I have finished the race,
I have kept the faith." ~2 Timothy 4:7

In 2 Timothy, Paul was nearing the end of his life, but he faced his fear of death calmly with the assurance that life after death was his promise from God. Christ had given him the hope of eternal life due to his dedication and unrelenting faith.

Often times, we are faced with circumstances that can be life threatening, such as being diagnosed with a dreadful disease such as cancer. Immediately upon receiving the diagnosis, one almost sees life flash before their eyes because we presume cancer may be fatal. Suddenly daily living takes on a whole new meaning as priorities are seen from a completely different perspective. If we were faced with death, would we resemble Paul? Would we face our fear of dying with the calm assurance that God is there, waiting on the other side of the finish line with open arms?

Christian life can certainly seem like a race, perhaps even an obstacle course, but we have to fight the battle to reach the finish line. Sometimes, Christians simply drop out of the race because they lose their drive and desire to continue their Christian walk. When the race becomes too difficult or the course appears to be all uphill, they lose sight of the heavenly reward—eternal life.

The race of Christian living will always be filled with hills, curves, bumps, and sharp turns. God never promised us that life's track was going to be easy and unobstructed. But as God's children, we have to continue to persevere, to run a faithful race, and to cross the finish line with God.

Challenge of the Day

Like Paul, are you confident that you have been faithful in your race to the finish line? When you have faced an uphill battle, have you asked God to help you persevere? Explain.

Day 87

Turning Bad Into Good

"This service that you perform is not only supplying the needs of God's people but is also overflowing in many expressions of thanks to God."
~2 Corinthians 9:12

From all appearances, Karen seemed to be the typical "girl next door." She had a good job, a nice apartment, and lived a fairly quiet, normal life. But looks can certainly be deceiving. In reality, Karen's life was anything but normal. She had grown up in a very poor, often abusive environment and had suffered many physical and emotional traumas early in her life. As a result, Karen had difficulty relating to others and avoided emotional attachments. She was deeply scarred.

Karen never talked about her past so no one was aware of what she had experienced. And sadly, Karen did not have a relationship with Christ. Then one day, Karen was invited to a neighborhood church by a co-worker, and there she discovered there was real hope for her. Karen gave her life to God and it changed her heart forever. Her trials and struggles had given her a unique outlook on life and she decided that with God's help, she could use those negative experiences to help others. She went to the pastor and asked if she could serve as a mentor for those who had suffered as she had as a child. By helping others, Karen found a fulfillment that she had never experienced in her life.

Many of us have had to deal with terrible experiences in our past. However, it's not the difficulties we encounter, it's how we react to them. We all have a choice–do we overcome our "storms" or do we let them drown us in despair? God has given us numerous examples in the Bible of people who suffered terrible trials and loss, but He used those people to show us how to respond to defeat. With His help, we can turn a terrible situation into something that will be a blessing to someone else. We can let God be the anchor of hope through our storms. And we can show God's love by using our personal pain to help ease the pain of another hurting soul.

Challenge of the Day

Do you know someone who has taken a bad situation and turned it around, making it a blessing for others? If so, think about what it took for that person to do what she did. Explain how you could do the same.

Day 88

By His Grace

"May the grace of the Lord Jesus Christ, and the love of God, and the
fellowship of the Holy Spirit be with you all."
~2 Corinthians 13:14

We've all heard the word **grace** for years, but do we truly understand its meaning? Can we actually define it? Just what is **grace** when used in a Christian context?

The word itself is complicated. Webster's Dictionary has about fifteen definitions for the word "Grace." And according to Wikipedia, "Common Christian teaching is that grace is unmerited mercy (a favor) that God gave to humanity by sending His son to die on a cross, thus delivering eternal salvation." What beautiful words those are: "unmerited mercy." In other words, God grants us grace even though we have not done, nor could we ever do, anything to deserve it. We are truly undeserving but through His mercy, He withholds judgment and extends His grace in some sort of blessing, a blessing that comes in the form of eternal life because of the sacrifice of Christ.

How thankful we should be to God for that grace! It has such powerful meaning to each of us. Grace, as well as mercy, came to us through our precious Lord Jesus Christ. We might ask, "Why did God extend His grace to us even though it is unmerited?" The simple answer is this: because He loves us so much. Jesus not only died so that *we* could live; He died so that He could live in us!

Through God's Word, we have been afforded a glimpse into Jesus, the man, as well as the truth He came to teach us. Because of His teachings, we have a greater understanding of who He wants **us** to be. Just consider how dependent we are upon the mercy and grace of God. That promise of unmerited mercy is the greatest gift any of us will ever receive. We are all immeasurably blessed, not only because God loves us, but because He loves us so much, we are granted His amazing grace!

Challenge of the Day

Have you ever given much thought about God's grace? Is there a time when you know that God extended His grace to you? How would you define grace to someone who did not understand its true meaning?

This Is A Test

"Love the Lord your God with all your heart and with all your soul and with all your mind." ~Matthew 22:37

If we had to decide which one of the Ten Commandments we thought was the most important, which one would we choose? *"Thou shalt not kill or commit adultery? Honor your father and mother"?* In Matthew, one of the Pharisees who was considered "an expert in the law," asked Jesus to identify the law which He felt was the most important one. And Jesus replied, *"Love the Lord your God with all your heart and with all your soul and with all your mind."* And if we read on, He said the second most important commandment is to *"love your neighbor as yourself."*

Jesus thought these two statements were so important that He singled them out from all of the other laws that had been taught before His ministry. But, let's stop for just a second and take a little test. And be truthful in your answers!

1) Do we always love the Lord with all our hearts, souls, and minds?
2) Do we always love our neighbors as ourselves?

Now let's check our score. Did we make a 100% or do we have some doubts about one or both questions? If we are honest with ourselves, we probably recognize the need for some improvement.

It's difficult sometimes to be completely immersed in God's love. Our lives become so complicated that it's easy to forget there is nothing more important in our lives than God. And what about our neighbors? Of course, Jesus was speaking of the "universal neighbor," not just the guy next door. Do we sometimes have a hard time loving others, even the unlovable? Hey, nobody said this test was going to be easy! It takes a little studying, a little homework, and some preparation time. But if we want to pass God's test with flying colors, we've got to have a heart full of **love**! By obeying His most important commandment, we are assured an A+!

Challenge of the Day

Is your heart focused on yourself or on God? Which one of these test questions did you find the most difficult to answer? Give an example of your loving heart.

Help! I Need You!

"Nothing is too hard for you." ~*Jeremiah 32:17*

With tears in her eyes, a young woman sat down to read her Bible. She often tried to take a few minutes of quiet time with God, but today she was upset, frustrated and maybe even a little angry. She was a devoted Christian, but it seemed that everything about her recent decision to sell her house and purchase a new home had gone awry. She was simply at the end of her rope. "Why is nothing ever easy?" she thought. "Maybe I should never have made this move. I'm just overwhelmed!" Ironically, she opened her Bible to Jeremiah 32 in which Jeremiah had just purchased a field and he was questioning the wisdom of his purchase. He was having doubts and he went to God for help. Jeremiah found peace in the fact that God loves us and sees our frustrations and doubts in difficult situations. Jeremiah allowed God to calm his fears and anxiety with the reassurance of His love.

Many of us face situations daily that cause us to doubt and second guess our decisions. When we make difficult life decisions, we try to make them based on what we think will be the best for all concerned. Yet, uncertainty and nagging doubts can creep into our hearts and we begin to question our wisdom.

In his time of uncertainty, Jeremiah said, *"Nothing is too hard for You [God]."* And when we are faced with complicated decisions, we too should turn to God and know that nothing is too difficult for Him to handle. Allow Him to soothe our doubts and calm our fears because we know that God loves us and He fully understands our situations. Let's pray for His peace and let Him help us through the hard decisions we have to make every day. We can be assured that He is there for us anytime we ask for His help!

Challenge of the Day

Can you remember a time when you allowed God to quiet your doubts and fears? Are you currently dealing with a situation where you need to turn to Him for help? Explain.

What Does God Want?

"Therefore, I urge you, brothers, in view of God's mercy, to offer your bodies as living sacrifices, holy and pleasing to God—this is your spiritual act of worship." ~Romans 12:1

Here's a simple question: Do we have anything God wants? Think about it. If we had one thing God wanted, what do we think it would be? Would He want our homes? Our jobs? Our children? Our money? What would He want that belongs to us?

Of course, we all know the answer to that question. God doesn't want, nor does He have any use for, our material possessions. But He **does** want something of value from each of us. He wants our **hearts**!

Here's another simple question: If we gave God our hearts, how do we think He would respond? Would he be pleased and overjoyed with our love for Him? Would He be thrilled by how we show that love through our kindness and actions towards others? Or, would He be hurt to see the condition our hearts are in today? Would He be disappointed with how we have let the world set the tone for our faith rather than His teachings?

If God would rejoice, then hats off to us for prioritizing our lives in a way that brings honor and glory to Him. However, if we think God would be disappointed, it is never too late to make a change. We have control over our lives. We should take a look within and decide—would God accept our heart as a testament to Him, or would we be ashamed to let Him see it? We all have the power to take charge and make our hearts something pleasing and precious in God's sight!

Challenge of the Day

How do you think God would evaluate your heart? Would it be a glorious blessing to Him or a sad disappointment? What can you do to insure that He would be pleased?

Day 92

A Box Of Chocolates

"And so we know and rely on the love God has for us."
~1 John 4:16

Most of us remember that famous line from the movie "Forest Gump" when he tells the woman sitting next to him "life is like a box of chocolates. You just never know what you're gonna get!" Yes, it is true that many times we don't have control over our circumstances. We can't always be sure that the piece we pull out of the box will be one that will make our lives perfect. We may bite into a chocolate that has unfortunate consequences that make our lives difficult such as illness, financial worries, relationship issues, or loss of a loved one. The centers of those pieces of life can be bitter and hard to swallow.

Of course, there are never guarantees regarding what kind of "chocolate" life will hand us. But how we respond to what we are given determines whether we live our lives in joy or disappointment. We've heard the expression, "Some people see the glass half full; others see it as half empty." It's all in how we perceive our situation. If we see the glass half full, then when life gives us difficult situations, we are still thankful for the "chocolate" we've been dealt and remember how blessed we are in other aspects of our lives. If we see the glass as half empty, we are among the unfortunate people who only see the negative things that happen to us. We can become consumed with the "poor little me" syndrome. Even a perfectly good box of chocolates just won't make us happy!

We don't always have the opportunity to choose our circumstances. Life comes with no guarantees that we will get the best piece of chocolate. What is most important for us to remember is how we choose to deal with our circumstances. With the assurance of God's love for us, we can be filled with the Holy Spirit no matter which "chocolate" life offers. We can overcome the bitter, bad-tasting pieces by holding on to our faith in God's love for us. We can be assured that whatever circumstance life hands us, we do know what we're gonna get— a glass full of God's love!

Challenge of the Day

When you get a bad "piece of chocolate" in your life, what do you think is the best way to deal with it? Which are you—one who sees the glass half full or half empty? Why?

In The Flow

"Whoever believes in me, as the Scripture has said, streams of living water will flow from within him." ~John 7:38

The word "flow" is an interesting word. Webster's Dictionary gives it several different definitions such as: to move as a liquid does; to pour out; to move like a stream; and to move gently, to glide. However, in our more modern vernacular, Wikipedia describes it as a mental state that relates to a person who is performing an activity and is fully immersed, focused, involved, and completely enjoying the process. For example, Millie exclaimed, "I just couldn't quit working on it; I simply couldn't put it down! I was just 'in the flow' and it was happening!" Obviously, Millie's attitude is just what Wikipedia described.

In John 7:38, Jesus said, *"Whoever believes in me...streams of living water will flow from him."* When Jesus said *"living water,"* He was referring to the Holy Spirit and He said it would flow from us if we believed! Do we fully understand that? If we believe, the Holy Spirit will flow from us! How amazing that would be–to be so centered and focused on Christ that people could actually see the Holy Spirit within us. What a light we could be to the world if we had the inner glow of the Spirit of God shining through us! His "living water" would flow from our hearts like a flood!

If we have the Holy Spirit in our hearts and truly feel the flow of His love, we can't help but be a shining example of His light. We need to let it pour from us as we strive to live our lives immersed in God's love. His "living water" can give us what we need to **stay focused** on Christ, to **be totally immersed** in His word, to **be involved** in serving others, and in the process, **find complete and utter joy**. We all definitely need to be "in the flow!"

Challenge of the Day

Are you "in the flow" as Jesus describes it? If not, what do you need to do to feel the Holy Spirit in your heart?

Under His Wing

"But let all who take refuge in You rejoice; let them ever sing for joy, and spread Your protection over them, that those who love Your name may rejoice in You." ~Psalm 5:11

The snow was falling so hard now, Teresa could barely see through the thickly falling flakes. Ice was clinging to the windshield wipers and she was becoming concerned. She checked on the baby sleeping peacefully in the back seat and whispered a quick, "Thank you, God." As she saw the lights from a truck stop up ahead, she heaved a huge sigh of relief. At least she would be able to get off this dangerous highway and wait for the snow to slow down. As she lifted the sleeping infant out of the car, she covered his little face with the soft blanket to protect him from the icy snowflakes that were falling so hard.

After an hour's wait, the snow stopped and salt trucks began clearing a path in the road. She wasn't far from home now, and she knew she could make it. God had once again protected her, and she and her baby arrived safely.

God is willing to protect us, too. Just as a mother protects her precious baby from the harsh weather, our God is willing to protect us from the treacherous conditions we experience in our everyday travels. The Psalmist tells us, *"God is our refuge and strength, an ever-present help in trouble.*" [Psalm 46:1] We just need to have faith that He is there when we need Him the most. What a wonderful and comforting thought that is! God keeps us **under His wing** like that soft blanket, comforting us when we experience life's storms. We need to allow God to be our refuge and our protector, our strength in times of trouble.

Challenge of the Day

When is the last time you turned to God as your refuge? In what way do you feel His presence as a protector?

Peace, A Fruit Of The Spirit

"But the fruit of the Spirit is love, joy, peace, patience, kindness, goodness, faithfulness, gentleness and self-control. Against such things there is no law."
~Galatians 5:22-23

As Kelly completed yet another job application, her spirits were low. She had followed what she thought was the right path: college, studying, and now even earning an advanced degree, an MBA. Why could she not find a position? Internally, she was struggling to keep an upbeat attitude and the motivation to continue the job search. However, she had thousands of dollars of college loans which needed to be paid, so she knew she had to maintain the search and find something quickly. Her stomach was in knots! Kelly yearned for success, but more importantly, she yearned for peace.

Research shows that anxiety is the number one complaint on college campuses. However, mental illness among children, in general, has nearly doubled in the last few years. Our society, not just children and college students, is filled with apprehension and anxiety, as we look to the uncertainty in our futures. From economic downfalls to moral decay in this fallen world, we are experiencing hurting hearts. We are all, at one time or another, probing and searching for inner peace.

True peace, one of the fruits of the spirit, can only be received from God. When we **trust** and rely on God, we maintain peace in all areas of our lives. Many times people turn to worldly substances and possessions, thinking they will bring them abundant peace. However, only God can truly bring us a peace that surpasses all human understanding. [Philippians 4:7]

Inner peace is truly a gift from God, one of His precious fruits of the Spirit. The next time we yearn for peace, let's set our focus on God.

Challenge of the Day

Do you have peace in your life? If not, what is your struggle and how are you going to identify a remedy? Create a plan!

Day 96

What Are You Afraid Of?

"So do not fear, for I am with you; do not be dismayed, for I am your God. I will strengthen you and help you; I will uphold you with my righteous right hand." ~Isaiah 41:10

At what point in our lives do we learn about fear? We certainly aren't born with it. But somewhere along the path to adulthood, as we experience bad things, we suddenly become afraid of all kinds of scary stuff. Stop and think about that for a minute...perhaps get a piece of paper and write them down. We don't need to include things like snakes and spiders or scary movies or the Boogey Man. Just think about things that may have affected us emotionally as we have matured. Here are some examples:

- Fear of failure
- Fear of rejection
- Fear of being alone
- Fear of a catastrophic illness or debilitating accident
- Fear of losing someone you love
- Fear of getting old
- Fear of death

Are any of these on our list of fears? Of course, we all have different fears we harbor as a result of negative experiences, but if we look into God's word, there are so many times we are reassured that we, as God's children, have no reason to be afraid. The Psalmist wrote, *"When I am afraid, I will trust in you. In God, whose word I praise, in God I trust; I will not be afraid. What can mortal man do to me?"* [Psalm 56:3-4] That's an excellent question! If we trust in God with our whole hearts, why would we be afraid? He is there to uphold us, to keep us in the palm of His hand, to protect us and to comfort us when we experience something fearful.

Now take the list of frightening things and tear it into little pieces because those hold no fear for us anymore. We are safe in the hands of our heavenly Father!

Challenge of the Day

Can you recall a time in your life when you were truly afraid? How did God come to your rescue and help you get through that frightening experience?

Stand Firm

"Therefore put on the full armor of God, so that when the day of evil comes, you may be able to stand your ground, and after you have done everything, to stand." ~Ephesians 6:13

A s he tried to guide and counsel her, the pastor said, "Kay, the enemy will do anything to steal, kill, and destroy your soul. You have to understand when that is happening and don't let him do it to you." As Kay listened intently, she knew the words he spoke were true, that the enemy had tried to destroy her. And she had allowed it! Her life had taken a downward spiral, and she found herself in a dark place. Finally, she realized that without God's help, she was headed for the trenches! It was time to get help. The pastor continued with the verse from Ephesians and stated that not only did she need to **stand firm** against the enemy, but even more importantly, she had to **stand firm** for God.

The enemy delights in tearing down our lives. He tempts us and we often hear two voices in our hearts and minds. Remember the old cartoon image of an angel sitting on one shoulder saying, "Don't do that, it is not the right thing to do!" while the little devil with a pitchfork and pointed tail was sitting on the other shoulder saying, "Oh, go ahead! It's just one time. Nobody will ever know!" Unfortunately, we often listen to the wrong voice which can ultimately result in disaster.

From a young age, we are taught the difference between right and wrong. When it comes to making decisions, we need to be aware of those soft little voices in our hearts that try to influence our choices. At times like these, we must think about standing firm against Satan tugging at our sleeve to disobey and put on that armor God has provided for us as protection and defense against evil.

As we are dressing ourselves at the beginning of our day, imagine those clothes we are putting on are actually pieces of God's armor. They are God's way of keeping us safe and reminding us that He is there for us. Let's not allow Satan the opportunity to steal, kill, or destroy us. Put on that full armor of God every day and **stand firm**!

Challenge of the Day

Can you describe two instances in your life when the devil showed up to steal, kill, or destroy? Did you stand firm for God?

Dare To Compare

"Each one should test his own actions. Then he can take pride in himself, without comparing himself to somebody else." ~Galatians 6:4

We would probably all be amazed to know how many times a day we make comparisons! We do it so automatically, we're probably not even aware we're doing it. Marketing experts have used this practice to make us believe their product is faster, healthier, tastier, cleaner, more powerful, more convenient, or will make us more beautiful than the competition. We also compare every time we go shopping at our favorite department store. We compare quality, comfort, proper fit as well as prices when we're trying to find a real bargain!

Not only do we compare things as we decide what to buy, we are also constantly comparing ourselves to those around us. If we are honest, we have to admit we look at the people around us and compare ourselves to them. We might have had thoughts like these: "I may have gained a little weight, but look how much heavier she is than me," or "My kid may not make the best grades, but he's really a lot smarter than her kid." We make these comparisons to try to make us feel better about ourselves. We can always find someone who, in comparison with us, will somehow be less acceptable than we think we are.

Although this is a natural thing for us to do, we need to stop and ask ourselves some very important questions. To whom do we think we **should** be comparing ourselves? Who should we use as the standard when we are trying to measure up and be a better person? We need to compare ourselves to Christ! He should be the yardstick by which we measure our lives. Instead of comparing ourselves to someone who doesn't measure up, let's start comparing ourselves to the one who was truly perfect. Why don't we **dare to compare** ourselves to Jesus because we will find His way leads us in the right direction!

Challenge of the Day

Try to think of some comparisons you make in your everyday life. Do they make you feel better or worse about yourself? What can you do to make yourself more like Jesus when you compare yourself to Him?

Ignited By Words

"The tongue also is a fire, a world of evil among the parts of the body." ~James 3:6

As technology has evolved, we have become a world with more words than ever before! From text messaging to Skyping, our lives have become filled with words, words, and more words.

As we talk or as we listen in a conversation, we should ask ourselves the following questions: Are these words true? Are these words said with a harmful, hateful or angry heart? Are these words slanderous to someone's reputation? Are these words spreading negativity?

Often, we are simply not aware of the impact our words have on the people around us. In James 3:5, James shares how a great forest is set on fire by one small spark, and He compares our tongues to a spark. Because of our human inclination to spread gossip, lies, or slanderous remarks, we often ignite a spark which can create a major fire in the lives of others. Unfortunately, some of those sparks can flare up into our own lives.

Gossip is one of the most frequent sins in our world today. Whether telling "a little white lie" or embarking upon a massive tale about a friend, church, or politician, words have the power to devastate and do irreparable damage to people's lives. Think of the pebble that's thrown into a lake. We have no idea how far those ripples extend and how many lives will be touched in a harmful way because of them. And when we twist details or share stories as if they were the truth, we are speaking Satan's language because he delights when we cause each other pain.

Let's think about this question: What do our words say about our hearts? James encourages us to tame our tongues and not let them be full of deadly poison. The next time we find ourselves caught in a trap involving gossip, we should seriously think about what we are about to say. Our speech is an overflow from our hearts. Let others see a heart on fire for God, not one that will ignite a fire of devastation. Remember, our words are not a tongue issue; they are a heart issue!

Challenge of the Day

Have you ever found yourself in a group of gossipers who were slandering someone you knew? How did you handle that situation? Explain how you will handle it the next time someone wants to engage you in the sin of gossip.

Day 100

Too Blessed To Be Stressed

"Blessed are those whose strength is in You." ~*Psalm 84:5*

As the minister concluded his sermon, he shared a story about a friend who, anytime he was asked, "How are you?" would reply, **"Too blessed to be stressed!"** Fighting back the tears, Anne thought, "Wow, what a concept!" Anne knew she was extremely blessed, but between meeting her deadlines at the office, planning her daughter's wedding, and keeping the household going while her husband's work kept him traveling for weeks at a time, Anne was totally exhausted. She was most definitely stressed!

When our schedules become so hectic and overextended, we can often feel completely overwhelmed; this can lead to feelings of anxiety, exhaustion and possibly even depression. In many cases, we have no control over what life throws at us. But before we let ourselves get totally stressed out, we need to step back and remember that God is there for us, even in the worst of times. We can't allow those issues that cause us stress to prevent God from being at the top of our priority list.

No matter what our present situation might be—whether calm or stormy—we are still totally blessed. All we have to do is look around us or close our eyes, stop and think for just a minute.

How long did it take us to think of the numerous ways God has blessed us? The next time we are having a pity party and we're feeling completely overwhelmed with our much-too-busy schedules, we need to take a deep breath and think about all the blessings in our lives. Then, smile and think, "Oh, I am **too blessed to be stressed!**" Share that thought with a friend too—it's contagious!

Challenge of the Day

When is the last time you had a pity party? What situations seem to cause you the most stress? Is there any way to avoid those times? Think of some reasons why you are **too blessed to be stressed?**

Acknowledgments

For each of these wonderful people, I humbly tip my heart and my hat. The encouraging words in **A Dose of Hope** could not have been constructed without the love and support of the "hope team." I absolutely cannot express enough gratitude to...

- **Kathy Straub, Editor.** Thank you for your abundant knowledge, extreme patience, and beautiful heart. Through countless hours, our "sisterhood" bond grew even deeper. I love you, dear sister!
- **Liz Young, Proof Reader.** With a God-loving heart and a teacher's "red pen", you were outstanding! From Hardinsburg to *A Dose of Hope*, thank you for holding my hand.
- **Charles Young, Proof Reader.** From one perfectionist to another, I thank you for reviewing *A Dose of Hope*. I appreciate your love and dedication.
- **Mary Bushong, Proof Reader.** From the classroom to the pulpit, you brought great wisdom and doctrine to our team. Thank you, Mary. You are a treasure.
- **Kari Underhill, Cover Design.** You are a blessing in my life. Thank you for your creativity, talents, and patience. Love you lots!
- **Ms. Ellen Maze, The Author's Mentor.** Oh sweet Ellen, your knowledge, skills, and expertise have been so appreciated. Thank you from the bottom of my heart. You were an answer to my prayer!

Mel Barbour, Karen Chaffins, Donna Dempsey, Judy Hart, Marty Hensley, Barb Nolan-Jones, Karen Owen, Debbie Reynolds, and Diane Underhill-- Support Team. Thank you for your encouraging words, helping hands, listening ears, and loving hearts.

My father and his sweet wife. Your continued love and support mean the world to me. I love you.

My children, their spouses, and my grandchildren. Thank you for believing in me. My greatest wish for you is to always keep God close in your hearts. I love you.

And last but not least, to **my wonderful husband, Curry.** God orchestrated our relationship and I am so thankful. I am extremely grateful for your love, support, and encouragement. I love you from the bottom of my heart.

To God Be the Glory,

Great Things He Has Done!

About the Author

Speaker | Author | Teacher | Survivor | Motivator

Sarah Meece had survived plenty of devastating experiences in her lifetime: the death of her mother when Sarah was just 13, a traumatic divorce, and even breast cancer. Somehow, she had managed to weather all of these hardships, but nothing could have prepared her for the terrifying and life-changing experience that came about as a result of a simple high school class reunion. Becoming reacquainted with a high school sweetheart soon led to romance and an optimistic future. But when nagging doubts convinced Sarah that marriage was a mistake, their relationship went from romance to unspeakable violence; ultimately involving the FBI, Secret Service, ATF Specialists and the Witness Protection Program. Sarah's story of attempted murder and a murder-for-hire plot is a story that conveys her unshakeable faith in God. Her shocking and compelling story will give your audiences an unforgettable journey into what it means to be a true survivor through faith and forgiveness.

Sarah has been inspiring individuals of all ages for years. She has traveled extensively, addressing a variety of audiences with her inspirational messages.

Interested in booking Sarah for your next event? Visit her website at www.sarahmeece.com or contact her directly at skmeece@gmail.com.

May God Bless!

www.sarahmeece.com